OLD MAN TROUBLE

OLD MAN TROUBLE

Ernest Marke

Weidenfeld and Nicolson
London

© 1975 Ernest Marke

All rights reserved. No part of this publication may be reproduced, stored in a retrieval system, or transmitted, in any form or by any means, electronic, mechanical, photocopying, recording or otherwise, without the prior permission of the copyright owner.

ISBN 297 76913 8

Printed in Great Britain by
Bristol Typesetting Co. Ltd, Bristol

CONTENTS

1. Early Days 9
2. America 40
3. A Brush with the Law 51
4. Return to America 62
5. In and Out of Trouble 84
6. My Life as a Crocuser 98
7. Soho Days 118
8. The End of the Road 147
9. I Settle Down 156

Dedicated to my devoted and loyal wife Elsie, sons and daughters Garry, Angela, Russell, Lorraine and Andrew, who all through the difficult years have been my inspiration.

INTRODUCTION

When I was a little boy back home I once saw two old men in rags leaning cross-legged against a wall, each with an old clay-pipe stuck in his mouth.

'Man,' said one to the other, ' you can't run away from trouble no more 'an you can run away from death . . . sometimes you get a li'l break, mos' times you get none.'

The other commented sadly, ' Yes, dat much is true, it's all in de Book. What will be will be. But when you's *Black* de trouble gets mountin' 'igher an' 'igher all de time an' you wonder when it's gonna stop.'

I didn't understand what they meant. But I knew that I also was black, and I wondered . . .

The first law of nature is self defence. If, in my youth, the inhabitants of this country had been as tolerant in their attitudes towards blacks as they are today there would have been no cause for my violent actions in the past. Before passing judgement put yourself in my position.

Not being an important person, to draw a full and convincing picture in this autobiography I have written it with dialogue which might not be word for word as was spoken at that time, but nevertheless it is as I remember it. And everything I have written is true.

Ernest Marke
London 1974

I
EARLY DAYS

It was twelve noon, eight bells were striking on the bridge that Sunday in April 1917. The second steward and I were singing:

We haven't seen the Kaiser for a hell of a while,
We haven't seen the Kaiser for a while.
He's gone to France to see what they're doing,
His fortieth Southland will be his bloody ruin,
We haven't seen the ...

Suddenly there was a terrific bang and the ship shuddered. We heard the ship's whistle blow the signal for all hands to muster to the lifeboats. A torpedo had scored a direct hit on the port bow.

The ship was going down fast, headway, so fast that the door of our cabin, which a moment before was facing astern, was now nearly facing skyward. We were trapped. While I was adjusting my lifebelt the second steward was balancing on one of the drawers, making a vicious attempt to open the door which was now nearly above us. After what seemed like hours it flew open.

The sea was rushing in, the lifeboats were away. There was only one thing to do. We jumped overboard. I couldn't swim but it made no difference because the sea was rough. Soon I was being tossed about by the mighty waves. Occasionally through the waves I caught a glimpse of a lifeboat. The second steward was out of sight and everything was racing through my mind. So this is the end, I thought. I'd always longed to see Great Britain: London, Buckingham Palace, the Houses of Parliament, the Bloody Tower and all those other places I'd read about; now I was never going to see them.

Remarkable how things sometimes turn out, I told myself: you make up your mind to do something and then – bang! – everything goes west. And though I had every reason to believe I was about to die, I wasn't in the least terrified. I was simply afraid and disappointed. To die right there in the middle of the Bay of Biscay, wet and cold at the tender age of fourteen, wasn't in my reckoning. Certainly not! Things like that could happen only to other people.

Another wave brought a lifeboat into view, but the waves were as high as mountains and I wondered whether the people in it could see me, let alone fish me out under such terrible conditions. I began to hope desperately that it was all a dream. Everything, every incident in my life, flashed before my eyes.

Then I felt a bump. The next thing I knew I was lying inside the chief officer's lifeboat. Among other members of the ship's crew in the boat was the chief steward, who had discovered me hiding among some crates aboard the ship – the SS *Adansi* of the Elder Dempster line – twelve hours from Freetown.

My name is Ernest Charles Melvin Patrick Ekundio Marke. I was born in Freetown, Sierra Leone. My father, a merchant, was a Sierra Leonean. My mother, however, was a Nigerian, hence the Nigerian name Ekundio – it means joy after sorrow – because my mother lost a son the day before I was born. As she was the first cousin of the Alake (king) of Abeokuta, one could say I have royal blood in my veins though it doesn't affect me and never has done; what did affect me was the blood of adventure, something which I have carried all my life. And hand in hand with this has come Old Man Trouble, a monster who stuck to me like glue for forty years.

It all began when I was eleven years old. Benjie Renner, Joe Lambert and I were classmates at St Edward's School. Joe and I were of the same age, and had been bosom pals ever since I could remember; Benjie, who was three years older and a bully, had forced his companionship on us. Joe and I resented this but were too frightened to say or do anything about it.

I had just returned to school after a week in bed with a fever, to find that my class had been taught a new mathematical theory. Because I was afraid of losing my position as top boy of the class – a position I held dear – I was very keen to understand the way the theory worked. As we three were passing through Victoria Park on our way home from school that afternoon, I stopped and sat down on the grass and asked Joe to sit beside me and help me with the intricacies of the sum. Benjie, who never took his lessons seriously and hated others who did, became aggressive and kept interfering.

This went on until I lost my temper and forgetting my fear of him, pushed him off. That started the fight. He pushed me flat on my back, sat on my stomach and with one hand throttling me began pummelling me with his fist. Joe tried to pull him away but he snarled at him and threatened him. Being timid, poor Joe could do nothing else but stand aside looking confused.

In desperation I pulled out the little penknife I'd always carried for the purpose of cutting rubber stamps, which was my hobby. I threatened him. But this did not deter him, instead his punches became harder. I then became frantic and started stabbing him. He loosened his grip.

But by this time I had gone berserk. I reversed the position, sat on him and kept on stabbing for all I was worth. If two men hadn't happened to be passing by and restrained me I would certainly have become a murderer.

One of the men sent Joe running to the hospital to get help for Benjie, while the other dragged me to the police station. I was asked for my name and address, which I stubbornly refused to give for fear of my mother being informed. I hoped they wouldn't look through my books, all of which were plastered with the information they wanted, printed with one of my home-made rubber stamps. They didn't look.

And because I'd refused to comply they locked me up in a cell the whole night with a drunk who frightened the life out of me with his grunting, shouting and grimacing. But even then the thought of what my mother would do to me when she found out what I'd done was more frightening.

By the morning, however, she had found out what had happened. And soon I was taken before the magistrate who, after finding all the facts, decided to bind me over with a warning. But my mother, still furious, insisted I should be given a good flogging.

The magistrate then ordered twelve strokes of the birch. My mother was soon to find I was going to get more than she'd bargained for.

I was stripped naked, held down on a bench by four policemen, and severely whipped by another of them under the supervision of the sergeant in charge. After the first six strokes my back and buttocks had become raw and bleeding to my mother's astonishment. And now she was pleading with the sergeant to stop the whipping. But it was too late. In the words of the sergeant: 'Madam, the judge's order must be executed.' And so it was.

For two weeks after the whipping I found it painful to lie on my back. But the worst was to come. On my return to school the boys had given me a nickname, 'Devil's Angel', which I resented strongly, thereby causing me to get into more fights. And now the priests of my church had turned against me and wouldn't let me serve at Mass any more; this hurt me more than ever, for I was a favourite altar boy before the fight with Benjie.

At football, my favourite game, I was often purposely tripped even by my own side. Frustrated, I begged my mother over and over again to remove me from St Edward's. But she steadfastly refused.

This treatment seemed very harsh, but in those days the discipline for children was strict in Sierra Leone. Fighting another person with a weapon was considered cowardly; anyone who did so would never be forgiven. So I wasn't forgiven – not even by my own mother, who never stopped reminding me of it. After three years I could stand it no longer and stowed away on the ss *Adansi* for England. And thus it was that I came to be shipwrecked and was dragged out of the raging seas.

I wiped the sea-water away from my face, and looked around. 'Oh, oh. What's this creature alongside the boat – a whale?'

I asked myself. Then I realized it was a German submarine. Two sailors were standing on either side of an officer in the tower, the officer asking questions in a commanding voice: 'Which of you is the captain? What has happened to him? What's his name? What was the tonnage of your ship? What cargo were you carrying?'

The chief mate in our lifeboat was doing the answering, but I was too impressed with the vessel to listen to his replies. 'So this is what they call a submarine,' I said to myself. 'So small in comparison to our ship and yet it sank us. Travelling underneath the sea like a fish with human beings inside it. These Germans must be very clever!'

After the questions, all of which seemed ridiculous to me, the submarine dived and disappeared under the sea. By this time our ship had disappeared completely and we were left on our own. Night came and then Monday morning. Not a ship in sight. When the first ration of biscuit and water was distributed we found that Freeman, the leading stoker, was dead. He had been having a bath when the torpedo hit us; he had panicked, jumped into the lifeboat naked and died of exposure and shock. This was no place for an inquest. He was dumped overboard.

Night came again and then Tuesday and still nothing was in sight. The sea had become calm but it was very cold. Then came Wednesday, then Thursday, and still nothing. Night fell again.

In the early hours of Friday morning a dark shape dimly appeared about three hundred yards away.

'What is it? A ship? Is it one of ours? Is it a surfaced submarine?'

'Shall we give it a signal?' asked someone.

Through all this excitement I kept quiet. What could I say? But I did make a prayer by myself. I prayed like I'd never prayed before. 'Please God, thou omnipotent! If this object is not a British ship then change it to one.'

Our crew were spared the trouble of making up their minds whether to give it a signal or not for the ship had spotted us and realized that we were a shipwrecked crew; in no time she was alongside us with a ladder at the ready. And a British ship it turned out to be.

I couldn't climb the ladder as quickly as I had thought. Both my legs were partly paralysed and my feet were terribly swollen; but with kind helping hands I was soon aboard in a nice warm room, a warm blanket round me and a hot cup of tea.

Our rescue ship turned out to be a small, fast British submarine chaser. She took us to Galway, in the west of Ireland, where after a couple of days' rest and a complete rig-out, we were put on board a train for Dublin, then a ship to Holyhead and another train to Liverpool. At last I was in England.

After all I could still see Buckingham Palace, the Bloody Tower and perhaps even the king! But as it turned out, I didn't see Buckingham Palace nor the Bloody Tower, nor even London for that matter.

After a few weeks in Liverpool, staying with the chief steward and his family at Wavertree and going nowhere except for an occasional walk to strengthen my feet and legs, with his three sons as companions, things began to get monotonous. The family were very kind to me, but because of my swollen and aching feet which stopped me from travelling far I was frustrated and often became irritable.

At my own request, however, the chief steward allowed me to attend the nearest Roman Catholic school for a while, which brightened things up a bit. I also served occasionally at Mass and Benediction.

One evening while serving at the altar, there was a slight commotion in the pews. A woman had fainted and she was being taken outside for some air. When she recovered she told the people around her that she had seen a devil at the altar – me. From devil's angel I had become a devil.

There were very few negroes in England in those days and there were certainly none at Wavertree. This was the first time that woman saw me and I imagine I was the first black man she had ever seen. But why a devil? Why not an angel or a ghost? I supposed in her mind only devils were black. After a few weeks of this schooling and altar-serving business I began to get restless again.

One evening while we were having tea Mr Rawlings came home and told his wife that he had been offered another ship of the same line sailing to West Africa in a week's time, the ss *Gabon*.

I became very excited and hoped he would offer me a job as a pantry boy, or something; but when I asked him he said I was too young and in his opinion the Board of Trade wouldn't sign me on. I pleaded earnestly with him, but it was of no avail. He told me I should stay at the school until I was fifteen, even though most children in Liverpool then were leaving school at fourteen.

I became very miserable and decided there and then that I was going to find the *Gabon*. I played truant the very next day and spent the whole day trying to find the docks. When I did I was very disappointed! I'd never thought that there were so many docks and so many ships in the whole world.

But I found the *Gabon*; I also found out the exact day and time she was due to sail. I decided I would get aboard a couple of hours before sailing time and find myself a nice, cosy place to hide; when she got to sea I should show myself and they would be sure to give me a job. This was my plan, which I thought was perfect.

But I was to find out it wasn't as perfect as I'd thought. The getting aboard and the hiding all went according to plan, but getting the job didn't seem to come out as I'd expected. Since there was no shortage of labour, I got the job all right and plenty of it; but there was no pay. I was also told by the captain, in no uncertain terms, that I would be thrown ashore at the very first port of call and perhaps put in jail.

Since the first port of call wasn't going to be Freetown, things were going to be worse than ever. All the money I had in the world was 2s. But something happened which changed the position.

At six o'clock on the third morning I woke up to hear footsteps running all over the deck, then a loud explosion like the sound of a big gun. I rushed out and ran towards the after deck, following a couple of the crew. Then I saw that it was our gun which was in action. Some of the crew were passing ammunition to the gunners. Shells were falling all around us. Strangely enough I wasn't at all afraid.

There was only one thing to do. I joined the ranks and made myself busy passing the ammunition along. All I could see was the splashing of water all around us caused by falling shells and the zigzag trail of our ship. This went on till nearly eight o'clock when a great cheer arose from the crew, ' We've sunk her!' It was only then that I knew the enemy ship was a submarine. I have never forgotten the awesome sight of nothing but the circle of oil where the submarine had been.

At that time merchant ships had only just begun to carry guns. The *Adansi* had not had any but the *Gabon* had been equipped with one just before we sailed. The submarine had shot a torpedo at us but our alert captain had seen it coming and manoeuvred the ship out of the way. The *Gabon* being a small cargo boat of about two thousand tons, the captain of the submarine must have decided not to waste another torpedo but to surface and sink her with his guns. Being a small merchant man with only one gun we must have seemed easy prey, but he was wrong; being young and impressionable, I enjoyed every moment of the battle and the swift revenge we took.

Anyway, having shown that I could be useful, I was informed that the Old Man had decided not to throw me ashore in the first port as he had intended. Instead he would drop me down at Freetown.

That was good news. If he could change his mind once, he could do so again; he might even sign me on the article with a job officially. But on reflection I wasn't sure whether I would like to cross that way again. I might not be lucky the third time: there were too many submarines for my liking. Furthermore, I began to think it wouldn't be a bad idea to stay at home again for a little while, if for no other reason than to see the stupid boys who had called me ' devil's angel ' eat their words. When they knew where I'd been and what I'd done they would respect me. As for the priests who didn't think I was good enough to serve at their altar, I would like to see their faces when I told them I'd served at a bigger and better altar than theirs. And in England! Now I could hardly wait to see their faces. Yes, it certainly wouldn't be a bad idea to stay at home for just a little while. Buckingham Palace, the Tower of London and all those other historical places would simply have to wait. They'd been there for centuries; they could wait a little longer. Why, I could even boast to everyone that I'd seen the king: who would know it was a lie?

As these happy dreams floated through my mind I thought that life wasn't so bad after all. Mother would be so glad to see me again she'd even forget everything I'd done. Yeh! Freetown, here I come!

But these things were not to be. Fate had decided otherwise; and it struck at our first port of call, Conakry, in West Africa, in the form of an old quartermaster.

Every time I had come across this man on the voyage, he would dig his fingers into my ribs, call me little Sambo and say things which always aggravated me. In the first place I never liked nicknames and worst of all I hated being tickled and so, every time I saw him I would try to avoid him.

The ship had just been secured alongside the wharf, and the gangway put into position. I was rushing to get ashore to buy some oranges when I ran into him. He grabbed hold of me as usual and started digging at my ribs. I tried to get away but he wouldn't let me. In a fit of temper I clouted him on the nose and there was a trickling flow of blood. He hit me back and we started to fight. He was no match and I gave him a proper trouncing. Unfortunately the captain saw this as he was coming down from the bridge. And there and then I was ordered to be thrown off the ship.

There was no baggage to collect for I had none. The chief steward tried to help but the captain, who was rather strict, had given his orders and that was that.

I strolled up the main road to the town. All I had was my 2s. I could speak neither Susu, the language of the people, nor French which was the official language. So near to home and yet so far away.

From Conakry to Freetown is only a few hours' sailing. But how could I get there? I could easily stow away again but definitely not on the *Gabon*. They would be watching out to see I didn't get aboard again. My only friend was Mr Rawlings, the chief steward, and I wouldn't like to see him involved in any more of my troubles. To crown it all there wasn't another ship in port.

Occupied with these thoughts I sat under a tree and cried my eyes out. I must have fallen asleep for the next thing I knew it was dark. With the exception of one or two people passing at intervals the only other living creatures were bats clapping their wings.

I walked down to the wharf again and found the ship had gone. Now I was alone and couldn't even talk to anybody. It was a moonlit night; I walked back to the town and sat under another tree. But now I was beginning to feel hungry and couldn't sleep any more, so I started walking again. Then I discovered that the trees, which were lined on either side of the avenue were mango trees. I was just thinking of climbing up one of them to see if they had mangoes when a ripe one fell right on my foot; I picked it up and found it had been half-eaten by bats. I soon consumed the other half. A moment later I was up the tree and there were ripe mangoes galore.

After I'd had my bellyful, I came down and had a good sleep under the same tree until the birds woke me at daybreak with their chirping. Later in the morning I came across a few people who could speak English. I asked how often ships called at that port and was told they called quite frequently; in fact the ss *Prahsu* was due any day now from England and bound for the coast.

When I strolled down to the wharf on the third morning, after sleeping rough and living on mangoes, to my delight I saw a ship secured right alongside. It was the ss *Prahsu*. I hurried aboard. And as I was following my nose towards the galley, where I could smell good food cooking, I bumped right into an African steward.

'Say, buddy, is there any chance of a job aboard this ship?' I inquired. 'I'm a steward. Missed my ship a couple of days ago, the *Gabon* from Liverpool, just gone down the coast.'

He retorted, 'Boy, why you tell such a big, big lie? No little black boy like you been Liverpool.'

I countered, 'I no little boy. I been on *Adansi* too. I get torpedoed.'

'Ha ha ha', he laughed. 'You big big lie boy! But com', pull punkah for me.' Pulling me by the sleeve, he grinned widely. 'Com', me like you.' As I'd never heard of the word 'punkah' I didn't know what he meant but I followed him.

He turned out to be the engineers' steward. As we entered

the mess room he thrust a finger towards a large swinging fan hanging over the dining-table.

'Dis be punkah!' he said cheerfully. 'When engineer com' for chop,* you pull punkah; if you be good boy, engineer give you job. If you get job, you 'elp was' dish, clean brass, pull punkah; das all!'

Well, one thing was certain: job or not I wasn't going to be left behind when she sailed.

I got the job. But I was told that because it wasn't official I wouldn't be signed on the article. And I would have to leave the ship at Freetown on her homeward voyage. But I would receive a good tip. I was satisfied; at least I would have the opportunity of seeing new places and meeting strange tribes of people.

I made myself useful on the trip. After I had finished doing my own job I would often go round and give the other stewards a helping hand with theirs, polishing silver and cleaning brasswork. For this I was liked by all, and made myself a lot of tips. Somebody always wanted to give me something – including the chief steward – shirts, trousers, shoes.

By the time we were homeward bound I was quite a dandy, and older. I had turned fifteen and had learned a lot about stewarding, such as serving at table, laying the table and making bunks. But as we were getting nearer to Freetown I began to get miserable because the ship would have to leave me there. I started making new plans. I asked the chief steward what other ports the ship would be calling at after Freetown.

'Direct to London,' he replied. 'All cargoes are for London.'

This was too good to be true and I immediately started searching for a nice cosy place to hide before the ship set sail from Freetown. It was certain that I would not be discovered, for by now I knew my way round the ship probably better than anyone else. And I could easily take enough food for the journey to prevent me from starving. My old dreams of London and Buckingham Palace came flooding back.

The day after this I was told that the chief steward wanted to see me. I became a little apprehensive and wondered if I had said or done anything to put him wise to my plans. Awful things began to race through my mind.

* food.

I could have been knocked down with a feather when I heard what he had so say.

'Ernie,' the chief said thoughtfully, 'you've made yourself very useful during the voyage. And now that the officers' steward has taken ill and wants to be paid off tomorrow at Freetown so he can go to hospital, I am wondering if you can do his job.'

'Do his job!' I exclaimed. 'Boss, there's no job in this department I can't do except yours and the chef's. I've tried my hand all around, sir.'

'No doubt you have,' he remarked with an indulgent smile. 'When we get to Freetown tomorrow you'll be taken to the shipping office and signed on. Your wage will be six pounds a month. How's that?'

'Very good sir,' I said excitedly.

I had to pinch myself after I'd left him just to make sure I wasn't dreaming. But all of a sudden I felt sick when the thought occurred to me that I might be spotted ashore by people who knew me and my family – what then? I decided that I would simply refuse to recognize them. It would have to be a case of mistaken identity for I had no intention of allowing anyone to bungle things for me at this stage. Anyway I hoped no one would recognize me. When my mother used to say, 'Never cross a bridge before you come to it,' I often wondered what on earth she meant. How could one possibly cross a bridge before one got there? Now I knew what she meant.

On our arrival at Freetown, the chief steward and the purser and I went to the shipping office, and to my peace of mind no one recognized me on the way although I saw a lot of people whom I recognized. The face of the clerk who was to sign me on seemed familiar to me. I became uneasy. He weighed me up for a moment and then asked cynically, 'Why does a little boy like you want to go to sea?' Without waiting for an answer he added coldly, 'How old are you anyway?'

'Seventeen,' I lied.

He looked at me suspiciously for a moment. Then he said, 'Don't you know there's a war on, and there are submarines around? What's your name?' The tone of his voice was sharp.

I had to tell him.

He scratched his head and pursed his lips a bit dubiously. Thinking my surname had struck a note I had to take his mind off it. I added quickly, 'I was born in Lagos. Anything else you want to know?'

'Have you been to sea before?' he asked indifferently, and added sharply, 'What was your last ship?'

'The ss *Adansi*,' I answered, hoping he wouldn't ask me for any previous discharge papers, for I had none.

'You're a liar,' he snapped. 'The *Adansi* has been torpedoed. You didn't know that, did you?'

'I know. I was on her when she got torpedoed,' I answered with quiet assurance.

He continued to write, then stopped suddenly as if he'd only just heard what I'd said.

He stared at me and demanded, 'Are you trying to tell me that you were on the *Adansi* when she went down?'

At this point the chief steward intervened. 'You are wasting time. Please sign him on; we are sailing soon and I have other business to attend to.'

Then the clerk asked for my discharge book. I told him I had lost it.

He narrowed his eyes. 'Next of kin?'

Having never heard of the word, I asked: 'Next of what?'

He became angry and impatient. 'Kin . . . KIN. Oh, never mind,' he sighed. 'What's your father's first name?'

'I haven't any father,' I answered truthfully. My father had died three years before.

'Your mother's?'

'I haven't any, sir,' I lied.

'Any uncle or aunt?'

'None sir,' I lied again.

He put down his pen, stood and glared at me. Then he stamped his foot. 'Listen, boy,' he roared, 'do you want to sign on this ship or not? Okay, you've been to England. Now you get clever all of a sudden, smart boy! You got no father, no mother, no nothing, huh?'

He banged his fist on the counter. 'Ever heard of Methuselah? He had a mother! I suppose you gonna tell me that you come down from heaven with one of them chariots of fire Elijah went up with, huh? Or maybe you just dropped down like that!' He snapped his fingers.

'No, sir,' I stammered innocently. 'B-but . . . well to tell you the truth, I was brought up in a Roman Catholic mission school in Lagos, sir. I never knew my people.'

He sat down again, lit a cigarette and after a short pause he glanced anxiously at the chief steward. He picked up his pen.

'What's the name of the school?' he asked mildly.

I had to think fast. Knowing that the names of most Roman Catholic schools start with a saint, I answered in an even tone, 'St Anthony's.'

'What's the name of the priest?'

'Well,' I said convincingly, 'we have more than one priest, sir, but the head was Father Dominic.'

After one or two more questions, he shoved the book towards me. 'Sign here.' I signed the article.

As I was going out of the door, I paused and looked back. He was scratching his head, eyes on me and looking puzzled. I pulled out my handkerchief and wiped my sweaty face. Although he did not have the power to refuse to sign me on, I was afraid that if he recognized who I really was, word would spread around and I would be pursued by my anxious family.

Two weeks later we were berthed at Millwall Dock, London. It was a couple of days before Christmas. Brrh . . . cold wasn't the word for it. I'd never witnessed anything like it in my whole life. It was so cold I could hardly walk upright! I was folded up all the time like a tired hedgehog. But with remarkable self-will and determination I decided to go ashore the next day to see the Bloody Tower and all its trimmings. The furthest I got was the West India Dock Road. Some kids were throwing snowballs at each other. One hit me right on the back of the neck and started trickling down my spine. I began to jump and twist all over the road like a witch-doctor doing a ritual dance, much to the amusement of the kids who then decided to concentrate on me. Snowballs were thrown at me from all directions.

After a few minutes of this Juju ritual dance I began a murder chase, a chase that really might have become murder if I had got my hands on any of those kids. I soon discovered, however, that I was so folded up I couldn't even run to chase a crippled tortoise. Besides, the street was so slippery I kept falling down; and each time I tried to get up, down I went again, sliding and twisting all over the street like a comedy contortionist doing a star turn, much to the delight of the kids and all the bystanders. I gave it up and crept, practically on all fours, back to my ship. That was the end of the Bloody Tower as far as I was concerned.

I never felt like being back home so much in my life. How could any human being tolerate weather like this and live, I wondered? That Christmas I was more unhappy than I had ever been: back home the sun would be shining and people in carnival costumes dancing to the music of guitars, flutes and washboards; and here I was cooped up in an ice-box.

How ironical it was that less than three weeks ago the thought of London had made me as happy as a pauper turned millionaire. And now – brrrhh!

We stayed in London for two or three weeks, discharging and loading, and then went back to West Africa. Four months later we were berthed in a Liverpool dock. The United States had declared war on Germany and all the big liners had been converted into troop ships.

I got paid off the *Prahsu* and decided to get a job in one of these boats so I could see what America looked like, especially New York. I had heard so much talk about skyscrapers and other wonders that I just had to see them. And since getting a job in any of these ships was now child's play, regardless of colour, because of the great demand for seamen, especially stokers, I signed on as a coal trimmer on the *Empress of Britain*. I chose the *Empress of Britain* because I was impressed with the name. 'Later, when I get back home,' I told myself, ' I can boast that I sailed to the United States of America on the *Empress of Britain*. That'll be killing two birds with one stone.'

The next time I found myself in New York, as I shall describe later, I suffered a bitter misfortune. But that first time I found it the most impressive place I had ever seen. And I was bitterly disappointed that I had to leave so soon.

I met a boy called Tommy McCauley from my home town and we became friends. He was smaller than I, though three years older. One afternoon, having nothing to do, we stood on the corner of Stanhope and Mill Street, discussing the wonders of ancient countries like Egypt and the Holy Land.

Said Tommy: 'I don't care where the hell a man's been, he's seen nothing! But if he's been to Egypt, Bethlehem, Jerusalem and all those places Jesus Christ used to hang around, now that man has been some place and has seen something! Those places are thousands of years old, you read about them in the Bible.' He went on, 'Now, if we could see these places we would have something to talk about back home. We may even see the manger that Christ was born in, you never know; they preserve these things, you know. What do you say?'

I agreed immediately. 'Yeh, you got something there, boy, I never thought of that but it's a damn good idea. Let's go right now and find a ship going that way. We can choose any ship we like now.'

As I was pulling him along towards the shipping office we heard the sound of a brass band coming from round the corner, playing a march I was crazy about and still am; so we decided to wait until after the march past, which turned out to be a troop of soldiers marching in fours. And before I realized it I was marching along with them, having absolutely forgotten all about our latest plan. And now Tommy was shouting for me to come back but I was too engrossed in the music to pay any attention to him, and by the time I realized what was happening Tommy was marching along with me. How far we marched I couldn't say, but we decided there and then to join the army. Needless to mention I was the influence behind this decision.

'It should be easy,' I said. 'There are posters all over the place of Lord Kitchener with a caption saying, "Your Country Needs You." That's us.'

'Yeh,' Tommy agreed half-heartedly.

We were directed to the nearest recruiting centre. While waiting to be interviewed, it suddenly occurred to me that one might have to be eighteen to be accepted.

'Hey, Tommy,' I murmured, 'I'm only fifteen. I believe you gotta be eighteen before they can accept you.'

'I was eighteen last week,' remarked Tommy, who had now accepted his fate. 'I have papers to prove it. I'll go first. If they take me they'll take you since I'm smaller than you; if I can be eighteen so can you – you've lost your papers, that's all! See what I mean?'

'Sure, Tommy,' I sighed.

Anyway, I was only asked my age, which I lied about and was never asked for any proof. That was that: we were in the army. We were taken to Seaforth Barracks that evening, and a couple of days later we were transferred to Preaseth Camp, Whitchurch, Shropshire, to join the 159th RDB (Recruit Distribution Battalion) for training. That was the finest thing that ever happened to me, for apart from the military uniform which appealed to me it made me feel grown up. The two months I spent in the army were very happy times. I encountered no colour prejudice of any kind and the feeling that we were all in the same uniform was a strong one. And soon I began to take an interest in boxing, which was to become very useful to me after the war though I didn't know it then. Tommy and I became favourites in the camps. We took part in every boxing tournament and lose or win we always gave a good account of ourselves.

But then the old Kaiser must have seen me coming for he decided to surrender. And soon I was demobbed and back in Liverpool. By this time I had lost Tommy. He had been transferred. On my arrival back at Liverpool I found that things had changed a lot. For one thing jobs weren't as easy to come by as they were during the war; finding the proverbial needle in a haystack was easier.

Thousands were demobbed and finding themselves jobless. I tramped the streets and the docks day after day, hopelessly looking for a job.

One evening, after my usual job hunting, I went to the African Hostel in Stanhope Street to watch a game of wappy being played (this is a card game usually played by Africans amongst themselves).

A deck of cards is shuffled, the dealer then places his stake on the centre of the table and says, 'I shoot a shilling' or whatever the stake is. Another gambler will then cover the stake and cut the cards. The dealer deals the first card to himself and the second card to the other man. All the other gamblers around can then make their bets on those two cards before another card is dealt. After all bets are made, the dealer continues with the deal. If, for instance, seven is the dealer's card and seven comes out first during the deal, then the dealer and all those who bet on seven are the winners. If, on the other hand, the second card is six, and six comes out first, then the other man and all who bet on the second card are the winners.

It was as simple as that, yet among the players there were so many grimaces, antics and excitement as each card was dealt that it became very amusing to watch.

While I was watching this game, two men came in covered in blood. Everyone grabbed their money, turned towards the two men and exclaimed 'Whassermarrer?' The men complained that they'd been beaten up by a gang of John Bulls. This expression was used by us not only to refer to the growing number of white men in the seaports who were blaming the blacks for the post-war difficulties but to all whites in general.

'Wha' you do for Jomble beat you so?' inquired someone.

'We no do not'in', we go look for job, das all.'

The man who'd been dealing the cards before the game was interrupted, barked out impatiently, 'Nemomind dem. Le's gamble de gamble! Dem go look fo' Jomble women, so Jomble men beat dem up; das all! C'mon le's play de card.'

'You s'ut up!' shouted another. 'Wha' you mean dem go look fo' women, dis two men neber look for Jomble women!'

'Dat's true,' said a stocky man excitedly. He beckoned to the others, 'C'mon we all go now look fo' Jomble, an' beat dem up!' Glaring at the two men, he asked, 'You sabe de'treet dem Jomble beat you?' Both men nodded.

'C'mon show we,' he growled, and again beckoned to the rest of the men. 'C'mon we go!'

Just then, the door opened and in walked Elliotte. Elliotte had always been a mystery to me. He was a small man, very quiet and unassuming, yet highly respected by all. All I knew of him was that he was from Sierra Leone, had just been demobbed from the navy and had lived in England a long time.

'What's all the trouble?' he asked quietly. They all wanted to tell him at the same time except the stocky man who just stood glaring at everyone and breathing heavily in savage fury.

After a moment Elliotte said calmly, 'Listen fellers, there are usually two sides to a story. How do we know these men are telling the truth? And even if they are, that's no reason why we should jump to conclusion.'

'Nemomind dem big Englis con-conlusion!' snapped the thickset agitator. 'We no get no time fo' dat; c'mon, we go beat Jomble!'

'You shut up,' snapped Mr Elliotte. 'You talk like the fool that you are. All right, you go out and beat up the John Bulls. Listen, you big idiot, this is a John Bull country; to every black man there are about five hundred John Bulls. What they gonna do when you beat them up? Just stand up and look at you?' He went on, 'In any case, two wrongs don't make one right. If these men are speaking the truth there are other ways to get even. You better carry on with your game for the present.'

'Ha-ha!' exclaimed the impatient dealer excitedly, mouth wide open and eyes rolling. 'Mr Elliotte is right! Des wha' ah say from de begin; c'mon, le's gamble de gamble! Ah s'oot s'illin'!'

I could only watch, listen and say nothing. Africans don't like youngsters interfering in their discussions. Though I'd been a sailor and a soldier during the war and perhaps been through more terrors of war than some of them, I wasn't yet seventeen. Therefore to Africans of that period I wasn't qualified to take part in older people's discussions.

Little did I dream that this was just the beginning of a big race riot that was to spread throughout the big shipping ports of England, Scotland and Wales.

But before I became aware of this grim reality wild horses couldn't keep me away from the streets nor the hostel, for by this time I had begun to get very interested in the game, or rather the antics of the players – such as the sudden jump in the air now and then by an excited player. And often while the cards were being dealt someone might cry out 'Bass' meaning 'Stop', which was the order when another bet was about to be made or retrieved. If the dealer ignored this command, more often than not the man might leap up in the air and land on the table, do a sudden voodoo dance and scream, 'When Ah say Bass, Ah mean Bass!' The second 'Bass' was often accompanied by a terrific stamp of the foot. If some of the other players happened to be moody at this time, a free-for-all would immediately develop. The African, like the Latin, is an excitable person by nature, but the African is even more so because in many ways he's like a child. Most of the Africans who played this game then were illiterate and therefore more childlike.

It was while I was on my way to watch this game two days later that I came across Elliotte. On his face was an expression of disquietude. He stopped me. 'Say, a young lad like you shouldn't be walking alone at a time like this.'

I didn't understand what he meant for it was early in the evening and I never go to bed before eleven; I told him so.

'Come along with me,' he murmured. 'Come and have something to eat at my place.'

I wasn't exactly hungry, but before I could say so he was leading me by the arm. And soon we were in his room.

It was a large back room on the first floor; a large iron bed was pushed against a wall, and in the centre of the bare floor were a table and two chairs. He beckoned me to a chair and asked me to wait while he went downstairs to the kitchen. Soon he was back with two plates of rice and snapper stew. We ate. And though I wasn't really hungry I thoroughly enjoyed every bit of it. He was a good cook.

After the meal, he began, 'You're pretty young to be in England. What part of Africa you come from?'

'Freetown, Sierra Leone,' I answered. 'Why?'

'I'm not gonna ask you a lot of questions,' he said, 'but I'm gonna tell you something. Big trouble is brewing and it isn't safe for any coloured man to walk the streets alone, let alone a lad like you.' He went on, 'There are a lot of John Bull gangs who go out beating up coloured people. I don't exactly know why, but it's getting serious. Within the last forty-eight hours over twelve coloured men have been beaten up in the streets. So watch out, son, and don't go out at all, except when it's vitally necessary.'

'But,' I protested, 'I must go out. I can't get a job if I don't.'

'You won't get a job if you do,' snapped Elliotte. 'The unemployment situation is getting worse and if there's any job to be had, you won't get it. The John Bull is the boss, he isn't going to give you a job and leave his brother out.'

We heard footsteps coming up the stairs, a loud knock at

the door and in walked a round-faced jovial-looking coloured man. He wore an open-neck shirt, and on the bottom end of one of his jacket sleeves were three little vertical stripes. I knew immediately by the stripes that he was an ex-soldier wounded three times. He turned out to be a well-known character called Joker.

'Hi hi, Elliotte,' he boomed cheerfully. 'I happen to be round your way so I thought I'll come up and say hello. Who's the little boy?' But before Mr Elliotte or I could answer the question, he went on, ' Say, whassermarrer with these John Bulls? The war ain't finish three months yet and they started beating us up. I suppose you've heard about it? What the poor black man done to them? We ain't no Germans, we ain't no Turks. What we done to them?'

'I'll tell you,' sneered Elliotte, pointing a finger at the stranger. 'We shoulda mind our own business.'

'Wha' you mean, boy?' croaked the stranger.

'I mean this,' said Elliotte seriously; 'in the first place we shoulda let them fight their own bloody war. Always remember this, Joker boy, a white man is a white man, no matter how you look at it. Whether they is Germans, English or even Turks, they all got white skins; don't you forget it. After they'd perched up their goddamn quarrel, what happen? They jump on us and say " F . . . off nigger, get back to your kennel." I tell you, man, that's jus' what 'appening now.' He banged his fist on the table. 'Bloody bastards!'

'Gitoutevit,' chuckled Joker with a grin as wide as the open spaces. 'All over the world, man, there's good, there's bad, you should know that, you been around.'

'I don't know nothing, Joker. I don't even know why I joined their bleeding navy. Can you tell me why you joined their bloody army, Joker? Look at you, wounded three times. What you gotta show for it.'

He paused and stared at Joker. 'And another thing; if you should walk out of this room right now together with a German and meet one of them gangs outside, you know what they'll do? They'll beat the hell out o'you and let the German go. They wouldn't want to know whether you'd fought in the bloody army, navy or bleeding flying co. You know why, Buster? It's because you're black, black!'

'Man, I never see you this way before,' said Joker with a chuckle. 'You sure got it bad. This thing will soon blow away I tell you; it's only them few cheap ignorant, lousy bastards who causing this trouble. Mark my word, man, it'll soon blow away.'

'Like hell it would!' growled Elliotte. 'We should do something about it.'

'Like what?' asked Joker.

'Well, we . . . I mean we could have a big meeting, say at the hostel, set up a deputation or something and see some of these high officials . . .'

Joker chuckled. 'Man, you taking this thing too seriously. I tell you it'll soon blow away.'

'All right,' said Elliotte, 'but in the meantime, I'm gonna go on my business as usual and I ain't gonna go out specially to look for trouble. But you see this thing here?' He dipped into his hip pocket and produced an ugly-looking automatic pistol. 'It's loaded! I've fifty rounds of ammunition to go with it and an extra magazine. If any of these goddamn bastard gangs mess about with me I'm gonna sell my life dear, very dear!'

'Man, you got it bad,' laughed Joker. 'Take it easy, boy, take it easy,' He turned towards me. 'I'm going home now; where you live, son? I'll walk you home.'

Months later I found out that Joker was my long-lost cousin who ran away from home before I did and to this day he's known all over Liverpool as Joker; only intimate friends know his real name. He is a very well-off business man today. He owns a successful club and a string of taxis and private hire cars which employ a large number of coloured and white people.

'It's only a few cheap ignorant lousy bastards who are causing this trouble.' Those were Joker's words. He might have been right on that, but he was not to know how wrong he was when he said 'It'll soon blow away.'

The race riot of 1919 spread all over the big shipping ports of England, Scotland and Wales with tragic results.

A few days later a young West Indian friend and I went up to Brownlow Hill on a visit. We saw a mob about a dozen strong. They started chasing us the moment we were spotted, shouting 'Niggers, niggers, stop them niggers.' A lady heard the shout, looked through her window and saw the mob after us. She beckoned to us, ran downstairs and opened her door to us and then let us out quickly into the back alley, from where we manoeuvred ourselves through other back lanes to the bottom of the hill by the Adelphi Hotel. No sooner had we reached the main throughfare when we were spotted by another mob. A tram car was going southward where we lived; we ran for it, the mob on our heels. I caught it but my friend was unlucky. That was the last time I saw him. I learned later that he was beaten unconscious and left for dead.

A few days later the riot was in full swing and I wasn't so lucky. I went out with my room-mate to the grocer's shop round the corner. From nowhere a mob appeared. We started to run back – only to find another mob facing us. We were trapped, and though we fought hard for our lives there was nothing we could do against so many. They beat us up mercilessly. Had it not been for some working women coming out of a nearby factory for their lunch hour, I would not have lived to write this story. The women rushed at the mob, shouting and screaming madly. Their screams and shouts probably frightened the mob away. We were both laid up for three weeks.

Liverpool, Cardiff and Glasgow were the worst of all the riot spots.

In Liverpool dockside, a negro whom I knew was being chased by a crowd of John Bulls and found himself trapped. He jumped into the river, trying to swim to a ship. He succeeded but even while he was swimming the crowd hooted and threw bricks at him.

Of course, the mobsters didn't get things all their own way. Some of them were badly cut up; negroes started carrying guns and razors to defend themselves. More mobsters got hurt in Cardiff's Tiger Bay than any other part of Britain, for Tiger Bay had the toughest negroes there were in Britain.

I am not an intellectual; I left school too young. But whenever I am approached and asked by an intellectual or researcher, what, in my opinion, was the cause of the 1919 race riot, I always say 'Unemployment!' Before and during the First World War there were, comparatively, very few negroes living in Britain, all of whom were seamen since there were no other jobs to be had. At the peak of the war, however, employment in factories became open to everyone. The country needed men regardless of race or colour. The coloured people took advantage of this, especially the few family men who had had to leave their family and go to sea for their livelihood.

At the end of the war things became different with the demobilization of thousands of men from the armed forces and the closing down of the munition factories. It now became scarcity of jobs, not men, with the demobbed men wanting their old jobs back and negroes being sacked to make room for them. But some of the factory owners, in fairness to them, still retained their negroes. Those who didn't get their jobs back immediately, began taking it out on the negroes – any negro.

Unemployment usually leads to unrest and starvation. These, in turn, make people look for a scapegoat. I know little about politics but I do know one thing. Any state that allows itself to become stagnant with unemployment is courting disaster. The mobsters vented their feelings on the negro who happened to be the small minority and the underdog. If the negro hadn't been there the confusion might have been worse. Perhaps even revolution. In a way, the negro saved the situation and the government by acting as a scapegoat.

The race riot in Notting Hill and Nottingham in 1958, however, was quite a different affair for there were lots of jobs to be had, with the construction of new buildings, post-war production and full employment. The end of Hitler's war, in fact, brought more employment in Britain than ever before, which was why so much coloured immigration took place. It was the government's solution to the problem of the need for cheap labour. The 1958 race riot was caused through sheer ignorance and hooliganism, which was partly instigated by a certain fascist element and it was only a speck in the pan in comparison with 1919. The authorities, the press and public sentiment in 1958 soon put a stop to it then, but in 1919 there were fewer of us and less people who cared.

It was during the 1919 race riot that I met a Nigerian fairground boxer called Wilkie. He introduced me to a white man called Hughes whom I was told had once been a British boxing champion, now travelling the fairs with his own boxing show. Mr Hughes put a pair of gloves on me, tried me out and gave me a job. We travelled most of the fairs and had to fight all-comers. I was only a bantam but most of my opponents were feathers and lights, sometimes even welters. It didn't matter much because the odds were usually in our favour.

If we happened to be cornered on the ropes by some tough opponent and couldn't get away, more often than not the bell would ring for time. But if our opponent was cornered, well, the timekeeper would simply forget to ring the bell. Furthermore, our opponents had to knock us out if they wanted to win; after all, the referee was the boss. I'd never had a knock-out punch because I couldn't hit my weight. (For some unknown reason I'd always been frightened of losing my balance when throwing a punch, so most of the time I had to depend on footwork and left jabs to win my fights: it was for this reason I did not stick to boxing – though in later years I had many a six-round preliminary at the Liverpool Stadium.) Wilkie on the other hand was a hard hitter who, more often than not would knock out his opponent in the first round. However, he was to meet a man much too good for him. This particular opponent was as tough as they make them, and from the start of the first round he had Wilkie in trouble. He was throwing punches from all angles. I'd never heard a timekeeper's bell ring so often at so short a time. But that didn't help Wilkie.

The crowd was shouting with joy and excitement. I heard someone cry out, ' 'it 'im on the eye and give 'im a black eye.'

Another retorted, ' Don't be daft, you can't give a nigger a black eye; 'it 'im on the bread basket.'

Everybody was telling the tearaway what to do with Wilkie. Poor Wilkie had to retire at the end with two broken ribs.

I decided there and then that way of making a living wasn't healthy. I quit.

I learned later that the tearaway was a professional.

Soon I was back in Liverpool. In order to ease up the unemployment situation and race tension, government-sponsored meetings for negroes were held with lots of propaganda stuff: 'British Guiana, the land of opportunity, gold in abundance and diamonds in various sizes for all those who are not afraid of work.'

I attended one of these meetings. A free passage with £6 cash was being offered to anyone who would like to 'jump at this great opportunity'. We were told that all those who wanted this chance would have to accept it now as the offer would never be repeated. All one had to do was to fill in the form and one would soon be in a land where the streets were paved with gold and diamonds.

Naturally I fell for it hook, line and sinker, fool that I was. Shortly I was in Georgetown, British Guiana, where I soon discovered that I'd jumped from the frying pan straight into the flaming fire. I found that jobs weren't that easy to get, at least not what I would call a job. When I asked about this abundance of gold and diamonds of various sizes, I was told, 'Yeah, there's some around, but, man, you gotta go right up the country miles away . . . People go and come back with nothing, some come back rich, and then again, some go and don't come back at all.'

'Don't come back?' I asked excitedly. 'Is it so good up there?'

'No, that ain't it. There's a lot of big snakes up there, man, big enough to swallow a man.'

'H'mm,' I nodded.

Snakes I never did like; gold and diamonds I like for what they can bring me but not enough to be too close to snakes. So that was out, dead out!

Soon I was broke and couldn't meet the rent. So, together with some of my destitute colleagues, we had to accept a job which we knew would be repugnant to us. We were sent down the river to cut sugar cane, the most detestable job I'd ever had if job was the name for it. A large nine-roomed house was given to us rent free, but we had to sleep on the bare, hard boards. We were paid according to the number of beds of sugar cane we cut down.

But none of us was able to earn anything the whole time we were there since we were all stony broke and hungry and had to eat most of the cane we cut down. Sugar cane for every meal, morning to night. The same fare we had on Christmas

Day, which fell a few days after our arrival; in fact, there was nothing in our nine-roomed house but sugar cane. Sugar cane was all over the place! Everywhere one turned there was sugar cane, everything one touched was sugar cane. We packed up the job the day after Christmas and worked our passage back to Georgetown on a river boat. I vowed that I would never touch another sugar cane as long as I lived. Fifty years have passed since I made that vow. If I live to be three hundred the vow will still be kept.

Back at Georgetown I had nowhere to sleep and nothing to eat; but luckily there were plenty of mangoes about. I changed over to that; at least they were more tasty and substantial. For an apartment I found a short mango tree by the sea wall and made myself a hammock between the branches with some old ropes. I found this more comfortable than the hard floorboards of our mansion up the river.

A couple of days later I got a job which took me to another part of the river to work for the Bauxite Company. This was a far better job than the sugar cane lark. It was tough, but at least one got paid and was given a food ration. The wage was 8 cents an hour, a free hut and a ration of flour, rice, fat and salt pork every week. At the weekends one could go across the river to the town of Wismer and relax with one of the many females who were ready to give one and all the love and relaxation one wanted for a dollar or so. But after a few weeks of this I got fed up and quit the job. I thought there was no prospect in it.

Once more I arrived at Georgetown, this time with every intention of leaving the country for good, come hell or high water! I found that getting a job on a ship at Georgetown was like picking gold and diamonds in the street. No captain would employ a man at Georgetown; if he was a man short he'd rather ship one at Barbados. I decided to stow away on the first American or Canadian ship but I found this very difficult. There had been so many stowaways from Georgetown, the authorities had now made it their business to search every ship at the last moment before sailing time.

I began keeping observations on ships in order to determine the right time to put my plan into operation. It was while I was on one of these observations opposite Booker's Wharf that a few of the crew of the ss *Canadian Gunner*, which had just arrived, came ashore. I immediately put on my best smile, accosted them, and suggested showing them the bright lights. My offer was readily accepted.

After the rounds I was invited aboard to have something to eat. I made good use of this by having my belly full, and on pretence of admiring the ship I spent a lot of time looking for a hiding place; being an ex-seaman it wasn't hard for me to find the ideal spot. Now all that was required was to know when she'd sail and gauge the time to board her.

From my hiding place I could hear the turn of the engine and the sound of the ship's telegraph. I knew when we were cast off. I knew, too, what we were waiting for at the middle of the stream. I knew when the pilot took over. I knew when he left us. I knew when the last telegraph order came through for full speed ahead. After that, I knew I was out of British Guiana for good.

I had been in my hiding place for eight hours and I must have lost over four pounds in weight during those hours. I couldn't even touch the meat and bread I'd taken with me; apart from foul water, the place was too hot and greasy. How I survived was a miracle. Six bells was striking as I came out. My legs nearly gave way with fatigue. I'd been in that bilge from 7 am and now it was 3 pm I staggered across the engine room, looking like an apparition; the third engineer nearly dropped dead when he saw me. A moment later on recovering he helped me up to the deck and then on to the bridge to hand me over to the Old Man.

The Old Man was pacing up and down the bridge when he saw me coming up with the third. He stopped suddenly, stupefied. He blinked, shook his head and blinked again. Without waiting for the engineer to say anything, he roared at me. ' What the hell are you doing on my ship?'

He stepped a couple of paces backward, glared at me, then took a pace forward, peered at me and barked out, ' I say what the goddamn, doggone hell are you doing aboard my ship?'

Before I could give an answer he looked towards the land, which was still in sight. He growled, ' You can swim, can't you? You better! 'Cause you ain't gonna stay on this ship another minute!'

He blew his whistle and a couple of AB's came running up to the bridge. 'Surely he's not going to throw me overboard,' I mused. 'He can't do this to me, it's murder!' But when the AB's arrived he grunted. 'Throw him overboard,' I couldn't believe my ears. Neither could the AB's. They looked at each other as if they weren't sure they'd heard right.

'Never mind . . . put him in irons!' he said explosively.

As the mate was going for the handcuffs, he shouted: 'Bring me the chief engineer.'

On the chief's arrival, he ordered, 'Put this goddamned man to work on the bunkers and see that he damn well works!'

As I was being led away I heard swearing going on such as I'd never heard before! I couldn't understand the reason for all that beefing. Surely he must have seen a stowaway before, I thought. I was soon to be enlightened. For the last three voyages stowaways had been found on his ship I was told, and there had been so many of them on that particular line, the company had made it a rule that any captain who brought a stowaway to Canada would have to pay for his keep in custody until he was deported. The Old Man was simply fed up. He had his own family to support, which was a big one too; and supporting other people's families, especially black ones, wasn't exactly his idea of fun.

Soon I found out the ship wasn't going direct to Canada as I had thought; she was calling at Cienfuegos, Cuba. I decided I would jump it there for there was no point in getting to Canada if I was going to be sent back to British Guiana.

Working on the bunkers trimming coal wasn't difficult for me because I had done it before. And as I could get along with all kinds of people everybody liked me except the Old Man, whom I always tried to avoid. When we arrived at Cienfuegos the chief engineer and third engineer called me aside and gave me thirty dollars between them and advised me to jump it. But, of course, I had already decided on that! On my first day ashore I roamed around hoping to find an English-speaking person who would direct me to a rooming house. But I failed to find one who spoke the kind of English I could understand. When night fell I sneaked back on the ship to sleep, knowing the stokers would keep my secret from the rest of the crew. At daybreak I sneaked off again with sandwiches in my pocket to hunt for a job on the British and American ships in port. I had no luck. This procedure was followed up the next day and the day after.

On the third evening, as I sneaked back aboard for my usual sleep and sandwiches, I saw that the Blue Peter was up, which meant that the ship was about to sail. Rushing to the stoker's mess room to fix up some sandwiches to take ashore I overheard a conversation which went like this:

'The Ol' Man's still ashore, trying to get them two out from the calaboose.'

'After the damage they done in that bar last night I can't see the cops letting them out. No siree! We just gonna sail shorthanded . . .'

I decided to take a gamble. I rushed back on to the pier-shed and took a position where I could keep an eye on the gangway.

I didn't have long to wait. I saw the Old Man going up the gangway, alone. And soon the longshore men were mustering on the pier for the ready to cast her off, some standing near the gangway. Then I saw the Old Man going up to the bridge, the chief mate going up to the fo'csle head and the second mate going up the poop. That was it.

I rushed up the gangway, up the bridge and faced the Old Man. Standing to attention with my seaman's book in my hand, I said, 'Sir, I believe you're short of two men. I came back in the hope of getting one of the jobs. I'm a seaman, sir.' I handed him the book. And for a moment he seemed perplexed.

I didn't tell him what kind of a seaman I was, that could wait. He opened the book and ran his eyes in it: 'Okay, get on the fo'csle head with the chief.' A moment later we were off.

I'd never served on deck in my life. My sea experience was limited to stewarding, and coal trimming. I knew as much of rope splicing and compass boxing as going up to the moon. I couldn't even tie a knot. But why worry – I could learn. Nobody was born as an AB. They all had to learn, and this time was as good as any.

As we sailed for the open sea I decided to go up and explain everything to the Old Man while he wasn't in a bad mood.

Perhaps he would understand my position, know why I had to stow away, and realize that I did not single out his ship. To my surprise he took it very calmly. He signed me on as an OS and promoted the OS to AB. All I had to do then was chip and paint and do odd jobs. In the meantime, I learned how to box the compass and was taught how to handle the wheel. By the time we arrived at Halifax, Nova Scotia, I was a seasoned helmsman. By that time I could also do some rope splicing. The trip was short but I've always been quick to learn anything that excites my interest.

On arrival at Halifax, I was paid off and held by the immigration authority but not for long. I was offered a job as an AB on a Canadian vessel, the SS *Watuka*, sailing to Santiago de Cuba and around the island of Jamaica. After a few trips of that, I decided to go to the States and join the American merchant marine. I went through the necessary routine and then took a train from Halifax to New York.

After many hours of travelling, I arrived at the Grand Central Terminal, New York, in the early hours of the morning. I booked my cases at the cloakroom and took a slow walk to see if I could find any digs in the neighbourhood. This was my second visit to New York. And my memories of it are not as happy as those of my first visit.

2

AMERICA

I came across a young coloured man. 'Say, buddy,' I inquired, 'do you know of any rooms to let around here for coloured people?'

He must have noticed I didn't speak with an American accent. Without answering my question, he asked, 'Where you come from, man?'

'Just arrived from Canada,' I said mildly. 'Halifax, Nova Scotia.'

'H'mm,' he muttered. 'That your 'ome?'

'No, I'm an African, but I've been living there for a while.'

'You don't say!' he exclaimed triumphantly. 'Well, I'll be doggone! You mean to tell me you's a real African? My – my! You's the first one Ah ever did see!' He went on, 'You know sump'n, you and me is gonna be good buddies – gimme some skin, boy.' He reached for my hand and shook it vigorously.

'Mah people come from your land many years ago, boy. But Ah bet you don't even know that,' he laughed. 'H'mm... you know wha' we gonna do right now? Ama take you to a eating place so you kin have sump'n to eat; Ah bet you's mighty hungry after all that travel.'

I agreed.

He took me to an all-night café. While we ate, he said offhandedly, 'Course this ain't no business o'mine, but for your own good Ah ask you; how you stand for dough?'

'Well,' I said, 'I have some money.'

'Hope you don't min' me asking, buddy, but Ah got to protect you; New York is a mighty mean city, there's more crooks around here than tea in China! An' you jus' can't trust nobody, no sir – not even me! See wha' Ah mean?'

I nodded and thought he must be honest indeed to tell me this.

'You gonna stay with me an' mah mother,' he went on, 'but before we go, jus' so not'ing goes wrong, if you carrying lotta money you better leave it here with Big Tony; he gonna gie you a receipt and we can collect it later and put it in the bank. Tony is a business man.' Pointing towards a big Latin-looking man behind the counter, he added, 'That's Tony – he owns this joint – a squarer guy you never see – ow' much you got?'

'I don't exactly know,' I said, 'but it's about a thousand dollars.'

'Phew!' he whistled, and then took a deep breath. 'A thousand buck! Man, that's big money.' He shook his head vigorously and repeated, 'That's big money, mighty big money! You can't carry all that dough around with you in this man's town. No sir!'

Again he shook his head, but this time it was with great and impetuous force. 'No siree!' he exclaimed and beckoned to the big fellow, who didn't waste any time coming.

'Tony, this is mah little brother,' he said seriously. 'He just won himself a lotta money in a crap game some place round the corner, an' we gotta go some place else. But it's a lotta money to be carrying about; you know wha' kind o' place some o' these places is. We want you to look after it for us till we get back in the morning and collect it and take it to the bank.' He added with a knowing wink, 'Dangerous carrying a lotta money about.'

Tony turned suspicious eyes on me and then on my 'brother'. After a moment he stretched a hand towards me. 'Okay,' he said mildly.

I wondered why the young man had lied. But shrugged it off after a moment. I pulled out my roll and counted it; it was exactly $980, all American, which I'd changed from Canadian currency at Halifax. Just before I handed the money over I asked for the food bill, but my 'brother' waved it aside.

'That's okay, I'll square it. Jus' 'and the dough over to Tony, an' he'll gie you a receipt.'

Tony checked it – they were all yellowbacks.* He wrote out a receipt which he handed to me. My 'brother' took it to see if it was made out all right. He nodded. 'C'mon let's go. It's time we had some sleep.'

He pocketed the receipt and we walked out. On the way home he kept up a running commentary until we got to a large house with an unlocked front door. He took me in and asked me to wait in the hall while he first talked to his mother. He ran up the stairway and disappeared. Soon he reappeared and beckoned to me from the top of the landing, he then led me to an open door and along a long corridor lined with doors. He pushed open one of these and we entered a large room in which were two single beds. Hanging on the wall were two large photographs, one of a middle-aged woman and the other of a beautiful girl, both coloured, whom he said were his mother and sister.

'Le's go to bed, man; when we get up Ah'll introduce you to mah mother and sister, an' if you wake up before me gimme a shake, eh?'

I was so tired I was dozing before my head touched the pillow. When I woke up there was a big fat coloured woman by the side of the bed, shaking the daylights out of me.

'Get up, feller,' she shrieked. 'You didn't pay to sleep the whole day. Your brother done gone and it's time you be hitting the trail too! Ah got work to do.'

For a moment I didn't know what she was talking about. Then everything suddenly dawned on me. Wide-eyed I jumped out of bed like a maniac, grabbed hold of her and howled. 'What are you trying to tell me, woman?'

I couldn't make head or tail of what she was trying to say. I grabbed her by the shoulders and shook her like a mad dog tearing at a cat. 'Tell me, woman, where's that bastard accomplice of yours?'

All I could get out of her was a whole lot of mumbling and whimpering that made no sense. I gave her a push and she went rolling all over the floor. Not wanting to waste time I put on

* $10 and $20 bills.

my clothes in a hurry and ran out of the building, heading for the café, which wasn't hard to find as I'd made a mental note of the position earlier on.

The place was empty except for a couple sitting in the far corner, and a girl serving behind the counter.

'Where's your boss?' I demanded furiously. 'Tony ... Tony ... Big Tony! C'mon where is he?'

Tony heard the commotion and came out of the back room, looking tired. 'Whasser marrer! Wha's all de trouble?'

'You remember me this morning, don't you?' I asked excitedly. 'My money, that's what I come for, my money.'

I dug into my pocket as if I was about to produce the receipt, a receipt which I knew too well I didn't have. The bluff wasn't needed. Tony looked surprised. He stammered, 'Whasser marrer with you, your brother been long ago and collect money.'

I ran back to the house, hell bent on getting back my money even if I had to kill the woman to get it. A crowd had gathered at the front of the house. I pushed my way through. As I started climbing the stairs, I saw that the place was crowded with policemen, the woman was in the middle of them trying to tell them what had happened. Our eyes met, she pointed an accusing finger at me and passed out in a faint. I was pinned down by a dozen hands, and because I was acting like a raving lunatic the more roughly I was handled. My growling and incoherent utterances didn't help matters. I was thrown in a car and driven to the police station, where, having cooled down, I was able to make a statement. They then brought in the woman, and for some time she was questioned and even bullied. But she stuck to her story.

According to her, she let rooms nightly. About 4 am a young man knocked at her door and asked for a room for the night for himself and his brother. She charged him a dollar and half, showed him the room and stood by her door and watched the brother come up so as to make sure he wasn't sneaking more than one person in. After that she closed her door and went back to bed. She went in the room about ten in the morning to clean up, saw me still in bed and was trying to wake me up when I jumped on her like a raving lunatic.

She was asked if she'd seen the young man before.

'Ah might have done, sir, but Ah can't swear to it as Ah was half asleep when he knocked at mah door. He is about twenty-six, an' ain't a regular. That's all Ah can tell you. Ah don' know not'in' . . .'

And that's all they could get out of her. Meanwhile a couple of police officers were dispatched to the café to question the proprietor. And though the grilling of the woman had ceased she was still moaning like mad, 'Ah don' know not'in' . . . Ah don' know not'in' . . .'

While I was scrutinizing the faces of coloured crooks from the police album (which surprised me as I had never believed there were so many coloured crooks in the world, since it was my first experience with any crook, black or white) the two officers came back from the café and told the sergeant in charge that the proprietor had admitted knowing the man, because he was a regular customer who was usually by himself. But he did not know his name. However, within the next hour I came across the man's photograph and pointed it out to the sergeant.

On leaving the precinct I was told to call again when I had settled down.

It doesn't sound plausible for anyone to be fooled and robbed so easily. But then I wasn't quite eighteen and hadn't any experience whatever of the mean ways of the world, nor had I met or even heard of a confidence trickster. I was soon to learn.

In England, where I first lived outside of my own country, all the coloured people stuck together. I might have been suspicious of the man if he had been white. But I never dreamt that a negro would steal from another outside of Africa or the West Indies where negroes are the majority. I thought he was only trying to help me, being of the same ancestral stock in a foreign land. I couldn't see him as an American. I saw him only as a negro.

With the exception of a little loose change, every penny I'd worked hard for and saved including what I'd won on the poker games on board, had gone, nowhere to go and no job; furthermore I was in a strange country, a total stranger. I thought of my last shipmates who often said I was the luckiest man in the world, simply because I was a better poker player. Lucky, eh, I thought; they should see me now.

When I left the police station my first thoughts were to go straight to the Grand Central Terminal, collect my luggage, look for the nearest pawn shop, raise some money for my keep and start hunting for a job. But suddenly an awful thought flashed through my mind: what if he had stolen my seaman's book and entry permit which was enclosed in the book together with the cloakroom ticket? Without a ticket I couldn't claim my luggage; with no book I couldn't get a ship. Anxiously I dipped into the inside pocket of my jacket. To my relief the book was there. But my fingers trembled like streamers in a strong wind, as I tried to open it to see if everything was in order. At last I was saved. I took a deep breath and thanked God.

Remarkable! Less than an hour before I'd felt like a doomed man sentenced to death and now I felt reprieved. Though I'd only about forty cents left from nearly a thousand bucks, things seemed different all of a sudden.

I've always been religious like my relatives back home. I'd believed in God always, so perhaps it was this belief that made things so different so soon after the terrible shock I'd had. Furthermore a very strange thing was soon to happen, which to me was a miracle. Instead of going direct for my baggage as I'd planned, something seemed to lead me in another direction. I wasn't quite conscious of what I was doing or where I was going but I kept going just like a man in a trance.

Suddenly I became conscious of where I was. Right in front of me was a pier; showing behind the pier were the two masts of a ship which, according to their position, I thought should be about seven or eight thousand tons. I stood looking at the masts as if I'd never before seen anything like them. Then I saw three sailors coming out through the gate of the pier, two whites and one coloured. All three seemed in a happy mood. They were coming towards me so I stood my ground; as they got to about three feet away I stopped them and asked if they belonged to that particular ship.

'Yeh,' answered one of them, 'we wuz but we ain't now! Why?'

'Well I . . . I mean, I'm looking for a ship,' I stammered.

'If you's an AB go straight aboard and take my job,' the coloured sailor said jovially.

'And if you're a fireman,' said one of the white men, 'there's two jobs waiting right now; she's sailing tonight.'

They were gone before I could say another word, but I was after them like a bolt.

'Say, buddy,' I shouted, 'guess you need a pass to get aboard, don't you?' And hoped one of them would give me his pass.

'Sure thing,' said the coloured man, 'but you ain't gonna let a little thing like that worry you.'

All three jumped in a taxi and disappeared in the traffic.

Now, I thought, how the hell am I going to get aboard this ship without a pass? So near to a job and yet so far away. Then the coloured man's last words began to drum into my ears: 'You ain't gonna let a little thing like that worry you.' After about five minutes of concentration, I remembered what I did in bluffing my way through the wharf gate at Georgetown in my bid to stowaway on the *Canadian Gunner*.

I marched straight across the road rolling like a drunken sailor towards the pier. I saw the gate-keeper eyeing me but I pretended not to take any notice of him and kept marching on, singing and looking very happy and unconcerned. As I was passing through the gate I suddenly looked towards him, waved a hand and said, 'Hi hi, Gate, everything okay?'

'Yeh, man, but take it easy.' He laughed heartily.

I was now on the pier and heading for the gangway.

The first man I bumped into as I landed on the deck was the chief officer, standing by the gangway and looking as if he was about to go ashore. I faced him immediately.

'Good afternoon, sir,' I said after a glance at the three rings on his jacket sleeve. 'You're just the man I come to see. I've been told you want an AB and here I am.'

I reached in my pocket, brought out my seaman's book and handed it over.

'H'mm, I see you're British,' he said, after running his eyes through the book.

'Yes, sir,' I answered. 'From Sierra Leone, West Africa.'

'So I see,' he muttered. 'We are sailing tonight. Are you ready to sail?'

'Yes, sir!'

AMERICA

I accompanied him ashore to the company's office where I was signed on as an AB. Then I went straight to the Grand Central, collected my baggage and boarded the ship with a pleasant feeling at the sudden change of events. Soon we were being cast off, bound for Europe.

'Remarkable,' I told myself, 'less than twenty hours after my arrival in this city I've been robbed of a year's wages, practically gone insane and nearly committed a murder! And now here I am sailing down the Hudson out of it all.' Surprising what could happen in so short a time.

Though I've been to New York City dozens of times since then, I never want to live there any more. I never went back to the police station, I had no time. But I was glad to leave New York when I did and not only because I was broke and destitute: I was almost certain that if I had seen that crook again I wouldn't have been responsible for my actions.

My new ship was the SS *Tongrier*, a Belgian ship of the Lloyd Royal Belge, chartered by an American company. Her crew was made up of nearly every nationality under the sun; but with the exception of two Jamaicans who were always quarrelling and calling each other 'nigger', the crew were the happiest men I'd sailed with. Even the arguments of the two Jamaicans sometimes turned out to be very amusing. One was always threatening the other with violence, but nothing much ever came of it.

The sea was mild and a nice cool breeze was blowing this Saturday evening during a dog-watch.* I was on deck, sitting on a hatch with four other men, listening to an AB strumming his guitar, when up came the usual argument between the Jamaicans.

'One of dese days me goin' beat you up so bad you never goin' rec'nize you'self,' said the aggressive one.

'Listen, man,' said the other dryly, ''ow many times you wan' me to tell you dat you's jus' was'ing yore time. Me's one man nobody can scare, nobody! Not even a ghos'!'

He turned towards me. 'Markie, boy, does me ever tell you 'ow me old Papi die?'

'No, I don't think so.'

---

* A two-hour evening watch.

He went on to tell me that when he was a boy he used to pay regular visits to his grandmother who lived in a nearby village. This village was separated from his own village by a cemetery, and every time he visited her he never got home until after eleven at night. His father didn't like the idea and kept on telling him that one of these nights he was going to meet up with a ghost on his way back home and that would be his lot! But since he was a lad who just didn't know the meaning of fear he wouldn't take any notice. Then one night, as he was passing through the cemetery on his way home, he saw a sight he could never forget.

His eyes became wide and he ejaculated, ' Right in de middle of de road wuz a ghos' crouching down! An' every time me try to pass roun' him, him jump in de front of me. Now me's one person who don't stan' no nonsense – not even from a ghos'! So jus' as me wuz about to push him off de road me see anoder ghos' behind him, a li'l one; dis surprise me, see?' Stretching his lips he added with a shrug, ' Well, me Papi never tell me dat ghos' does walk in pairs, see wha' I mean? So me say so loud an' clear.' After a short pause he asked in innocent surprise, ' Wha' you t'ink de big ghos' do when him hear me say so?'

' Not the slightest idea, man,' I replied, pretending to be very interested, one ear listening to the guitarist. ' Tell me, man, tell me.'

He pursed his lips. ' De big ghos' turned to look roun' to see wha' I mean. An' den t'ings begin to 'appen. Wow! When him see de li'l one him suddenly jump up in de air an' start running like a deer, wit' de li'l one chasing him like a lion! Markie, boy, you never see a t'ing funny so! A big ghos' like him frighten' of a li'l one less than half him size . . .'

' Shut yore lying mouth, nigger boy!' the other fellow snapped. ' Does you expect intelligen' people like we to believe dat rass*?' Then he got off the hatch in a huff, looking contemptuously at his countryman.

The storyteller glared at his tormentor. ' Shut yore big black ignoran' mout'!' he retorted. ' Me ain't talking to you, me's talking to Markie.' He again turned his eyes on me. ' As me

---

* Profane swearing used by Jamaicans.

wuz saying, Markie boy. Every time de big ghos' look back and see de li'l ghos' behind him, goddamnit, him jump up 'igher an' put up more speed! Boy, me never laugh so much in me life!'

The other fellow, now leaning with his back against the bulwark, stamped hard on the deck angrily and pointed an aggressive finger at the storyteller. ' You ugly lying nigger!' he roared. ' Laugh me eye! If dis is true, which I don' believe at all at all, de only reason you didn't run an' run de odder way as fast as you could go wuz because you wuz so scared yore foot wouldn't move!'

The storyteller gave him a look of contempt and again turned his eyes on me. ' Well, when me get 'ome wha' you t'ink me see!'

It wasn't a question but I answered, ' I don't know.'

' Lying dead in de middle of de room wuz me po old Papi wit' a sheet roun' him. An' sitting by him side, looking sorrowful like, wuz we li'l pet monkey name Jacko, wit' a table clot' roun' him shoulder.' He added sadly, ' Me poor Papi will never try to play de ghos' wit' me no more for him is a true ghos' now! Him couldn'ta known dat de li'l ghos' behind him wuz we monkey, who always wanta do wat people do.' He shook his head sadly. ' Him musta died wit' heart failure.' Suddenly he jumped up. And with simulated anger he thrust a finger at the other man.

' An' dis big mout' rass nigger 'ere t'ink him can scare a man like me wit' him talk! Him gotta lotta time to was'e! Him shoulda be in Alcatraz. Cha!' He then stormed off uttering some unprintable words.

But we all knew that soon the two would be slapping each other again on the back with lavish display of teeth and hilarious laughter. For the *Tongrier* was indeed a happy ship.

We made lots of friends in France and Belgium. The quayside was always lined up with beautiful girls waiting as we docked.

But all good things have a habit of coming to an end. The charter was over and the American pay which those of us who signed on in the States were having had to come to a stop. We were given the opportunity to stay on on Belgian pay or be paid off and sent back to New York. But because of my distasteful experience in that city I had come to hate America. I thought if my own race could inflict such injustice on me by wilfully depriving me of all my savings, what chance would I have with the whites in that country? I decided to get paid off and come to England since the British mercantile marines' pay was higher than the Belgians'. I knew that back in England I'd be fishing in troubled waters because of my colour. But there was no hiding place – not if I still wanted to make my living abroad.

I asked for a free passage to Liverpool instead of New York. To this the company agreed. I was given a ticket via Southampton.

3

A BRUSH WITH THE LAW

I didn't repeat the mistake I made when travelling from Halifax to New York by carrying all my money on my person. This time with the exception of a few pounds all my money was sent to England through Lloyd's Bank.

On my arrival back at Liverpool I found that the race riot had stopped as I'd expected and ships weren't as hard to get as they were in 1919. This was 1921. I'd been away two years. But the colour prejudice was still intense. In fact, I found that even some members of the Liverpool police force had become so prejudiced against coloured men that their behaviour towards them had become nothing less than hooliganism. This is no exaggeration. The incident I am about to relate may still be recorded on the police files in Liverpool. Barely a month had passed since my return to that city when it happened.

About 11 pm one night on my way home from a visit three men approached me as I came to Hope Street. One of them asked for a light and I told him truthfully that I hadn't any. A moment later they surrounded me and one of them punched me in the stomach. As I doubled up all three started throwing kicks at me. I knew I hadn't a chance. But as my anger had risen I fought back desperately and managed to draw blood from one of them. And just as I began to make a run for it I was grabbed. While being dragged to the police station, which turned out to be nearby, the third man walked behind and kept kicking me.

It was at the station I discovered to my surprise that they were police officers in civvies. Prior to this I'd heard of coloured men who had been beaten up by police officers in civvies and had later recognized these officers in their uniform. But because I had believed in the integrity of the police I would not accept it. It was a long time after my own experience before I could bring myself to trust another police officer. Since then, however, I've found that there are wicked and treacherous people in all professions, and the police are no exception.

Arriving at the police station I was pushed violently towards a bench. Dejected, I sat with my head resting on my hands. One of the officers who had arrested me pulled his truncheon, walked up to me and split the back of my head open.

I carry the mark to this day and no doubt I shall carry it to my grave. There was absolutely nothing to justify his action for I'd stopped struggling since we entered the station.

I was then searched. A loaded tiny Belgian revolver was found in my hip pocket. This may sound incredible, but I didn't even know I had the gun on me. Had I know I certainly would have used it with justification. The last time I had seen the gun was at Le Havre, France. I had hidden it in the hip pocket of one of my suits when packing at Le Havre, where I was paid off, to evade the customs at Southampton. On arrival at Liverpool, I had hung all the suits in a wardrobe to prevent crease and it was the first time I had changed into that particular suit. The gun was so tiny its weight could hardly be felt in one's pocket, and I had quite forgotten about it. In fact I had bought it in Antwerp, Belgium, simply for the novelty of its diminutive size.

I was charged with about seven different offences which were all fallacious, except the one of carrying firearms and ammunition without a licence. When I appeared at Dale Street police court the next morning another charge had been added: the attempted murder of a police officer.

They had 'discovered' a little dent on one of the bullets and claimed that I'd shot at one of the police officers; it was just a miracle the gun hadn't gone off; there was the dent to prove it. And if it hadn't been for the courage and quick thinking of one of the officers who coshed me and knocked me out before I was able to pull the trigger the second time, one of them would have been shot and probably killed. To prove their achievement the officer giving the evidence pointed at my bandaged head.

Race hatred must be a terrible thing, I thought. To be vindictive to a total stranger who had done no harm was incomprehensible to me. The only reason I was before that court was that I wasn't white. That and nothing else!

Because I was too frustrated and flabbergasted to say anything I simply pleaded not guilty. I was remanded at Walton Jail for a week. When I appeared at the court the following week all the other charges had been dropped except the major one of attempted murder. I was then told that I would again be remanded in custody to appear at the Liverpool Assizes at St George's Hall at a later date. I was asked if I had anything to say.

I shook my head sadly. 'I don't know what to say,' I said quietly, 'I am simply not guilty of this charge.'

I was then asked if I would be wanting any aid. Coshing a man and asking at the same time if he needed any help wasn't logical to me. I recollected while in jail the week before asking a visiting friend to get me a lawyer, which he did. But because the lawyer had advised me to plead guilty and I refused since I'd be lying against myself, we had words and he left. If that was the kind of aid they had in mind they could jolly well keep it. I felt it was a conspiracy and was having none of it.

I shook my head. 'No.'

I decided to defend myself when the proper time came. But until then I was determined not to say anything except 'not guilty'.

While incarcerated in Walton Jail awaiting trial, with nothing to do, I reviewed the police statement by memory, trying to find a loophole in their lies to prove myself innocent. Though every word in their statement was untrue I knew that lies from competent prevaricators – especially policemen – could be very damaging. And more so to me, for I had never been in a law court until now and knew nothing about police procedure.

The police statement went like this: Between 10.30 and 11 pm they saw me talking with another coloured man at Hope Street. I was very excited, waving my hands and saying, 'Me go kill him now, and if you no belief – look – I have a gun.' (I would never use such an expression. But they were unaware of this.) I then pulled out the gun and showed it to the man. And soon the man walked away. They then approached and asked me if I had a licence for the gun. I immediately jumped three paces backwards, pointing the gun at them, and then pulled the trigger. They heard the click of the hammer, but no explosion. Before I had time to pull the trigger again I was knocked out with a truncheon by one of them.

I had listened carefully to their sworn evidence and my memory was good. But not knowing I was entitled to demand a copy of this evidence I asked a warder for some writing paper. Then I wrote down their statement as far as my memory permitted. I read it over and over again, trying to find a weak link which would help me to prove my innocence.

I found three. One, the coloured man I was supposed to be talking to; two, the distance between the police and myself when I pulled the trigger; and three, the position of the wound on my head. First the coloured man: if their story was true surely they should be able to produce him in court; coloured people in England in those days were so few that they all knew each other in whatever town or city they lived. On second thoughts I presumed they would find a suitable excuse for not producing him. I decided that though I would ask for the production of the man, I wouldn't make a play on it but would definitely lay stress on links two and three. And since I had nothing to hide I hoped commonsense and fair judgement would decide.

When I finally appeared at the Assizes the atmosphere of the court nearly frightened the life out of me. There was the High Court judge dressed in a red robe and long white wig and looking very awesome, apart from others in black robes and shorter wigs, not to mention the twelve solemn-looking men who I was told were the jury. I'd never seen anything like it in my life. The whole scene looked to me like what I had imagined the real Judgement Day would be. The only difference was I couldn't see anybody with wings. I pinched myself to see if I was dead and found I was still alive, which frightened me even more. I looked round the court. There wasn't a black face in sight. Dejectedly I wondered what chance I had against all these people when even my accusers were white.

I could see myself being thrown into gaol for the rest of my natural life or perhaps even hanged. It would have been far better if I was dead and done with, I thought, for whatever the result it couldn't be anything else but horrible. I began to think I was a fool for not listening to that lawyer; at least I would have had one white man pleading for me. Now I was left alone.

Suddenly I seemed to hear a voice whispering to me that I wasn't alone. The imaginary voice was saying, 'There is a just God bigger than any of these people, including the judge. Do not be afraid.' And now I felt a lot better and all fear left me. I was ready to fight to the last.

After I had pleaded not guilty and the prosecuting counsel had finished his opening speech, a policeman started with his evidence, which was nothing but a pack of lies without one particle of truth. I became so furious I couldn't restrain myself any longer. I jumped up and cried out, 'It's all a pack of lies, lies, lies!'

I was advised to be quiet and told 'Your time will come to ask him questions and give your version. But right now you must remain quiet.'

I kept quiet, but it was very difficult to just sit and listen to such abominable lies!

After the evidence, I was asked if I had any questions to ask the officer in the witness box. By this time I had cooled down a lot, thanks to the two guards at my side who had been whispering to me to be patient.

I got up. As far as I can remember, my cross-examination of the witness went something like this:

Myself: According to your statement, you saw me showing my revolver to another coloured man on a street corner. Can you produce this man?
Police: No.
Myself: Why not?
Police: We made several inquiries but couldn't trace him. I suppose he's gone back to sea.

I was expecting this answer so I brushed it off with a flick of my hand. I knew that nearly all coloured men in Liverpool in those days were seamen.

Myself: Where were you standing when you saw me talking to this – er – imaginary man?
Police: Across the road.
Myself: What did you do then?
Police: We crossed over and asked you if you had a licence for the gun.
Myself: Was the gun in my pocket then or was I still holding it in my hand and showing it to the – er – man?
Police: You still had it in your hand. But the man had walked away. He did so when he saw us walking towards you.
Myself: Why should he walk away? Surely you were not in uniform.
Police: Perhaps he did not want to be involved.
Myself: What was the distance between us when you spoke to me?
Police: About two paces.
Myself: Were all three of you facing me?
Police: Yes.
Myself: Did I, at any time, try to run or turn my back towards you?
Police: No.
Myself: Are you sure of that?
Police: Er – yes.
Myself: Then would I be right in saying since we were all facing each other no one could've been standing behind me?
Police: Yes.
Myself: What happened then?
Police: You jumped three paces backward, pointing the gun at us, and pulled the trigger.
Myself: How many times did I – er – pull the trigger?
Police: Once as far as I know.
Myself: What was it that prevented me from pulling it more than once, when according to you I already had the gun in my hand – and the initial ad-

A BRUSH WITH THE LAW

	vantage by my sudden move in jumping the three paces backward?
Police:	We were too quick for you.
Myself:	Perhaps so. But not being English would I be right in saying that pace is a certain rate of progression?
Police:	Yes.
Myself:	Am I right in saying that jump is to spring or move with a sudden start?
Police:	Yes.
Myself:	And jumping three paces back could mean a distance of five feet or more between us?
Police:	I suppose so.
Myself:	Supposition is not always a fact. Am I right?
Police:	Yes.
Myself:	You have admitted that the distance between us when I am supposed to have pulled the trigger must have been at least five feet. Are you trying to tell the court that at this distance you were quick enough to jump me and cosh me directly on the back of the head when other parts of the head would have been more convenient to hit?

The witness paused and seemed to be weighing up the question. Then he answered:

	Come to think of it, the distance between us couldn't have been that wide because we were moving towards you at the same time as you were moving backwards.
Myself:	But since my jumping back was sudden and therefore not anticipated by you, wasn't it possible that the distance between us could have been just about that – if not more?
Police:	We always expect sudden moves from people we're about to question or arrest.
Myself:	Not being a policeman or a criminal, I wouldn't know about that. But you do admit the blow was struck directly on the back of my head and was done even before I could have another opportunity of performing the simple act of pulling the trigger the second time – when the gun was

	already pointing at you, according to your evidence?
Police:	Yes. But it wasn't I who struck the blow.
Myself:	Are you surprised to know that the wound is directly on the back of my head?
Police:	One does not aim at any particular part of the head when having to use a truncheon.
Myself:	I quite agree. And if the man coshed was sitting with bowed head the blow would fall automatically on the back of the head would it not?
Police:	Eh – yes. But he would be unlikely to be sitting down.
Myself:	Perhaps. But let's get back to the revolver. Was it defective in anyway?
Police:	It didn't go off at the first pull of the trigger.
Myself:	So by your quick action you prevented me from pulling the trigger a second time.

I thrust my right fist forward, fore finger curved:

Imagine my fist is a revolver, my finger on the trigger. Watch me pull twice at the trigger.

I pulled twice at the imaginary trigger.

Now watch for the next move.

I glanced at the judge and jury and then performed a little action, as far as space permitted, by trying to jump a few paces and pretending to hit an imaginary opponent on the back of the head – to the surprise of my guards, who probably thought I was trying to run off and made a move to stop me.

	Surely you are not trying to tell the court that the second move is quicker than the first?
Police:	That depends on the performers. One's action is as quick as the other allows him to be.
Myself:	Then you are telling the court that – in this particular case – taking five paces is quicker than pulling a trigger twice. Remarkable!

I looked at the judge, then at the jury and back at him.

That is all.

Practically the same questions were asked to the other two. But to the one who was supposed to have struck the blow and grabbed the gun, I added:

Forgetting the increase in distance between us by

	the alleged jumping three paces, you do, however, agree that I was at least two paces away from you when I was supposed to have pulled the trigger?
Police:	Yes.
Myself:	You rushed and hit me on the head before I could pull the trigger again and then wrenched the revolver out of my hand?
Police:	Yes.
Myself:	Now, since the wound is directly on the back of my head, can you explain to the court how you managed to perform this extraordinary feat of contortion before I had a chance of pulling the trigger more than once, when, according to your sworn evidence, I was facing you with a loaded gun in my hand, my finger on the trigger, attempting to commit a wilful murder – and I was, according to your own statement, at least two paces away from you?
Police:	I didn't give you a chance.
Myself:	Do you agree that there wasn't a wound on any other part of my head apart from that on the back of my head?
Police:	Yes.
Myself:	Since I did not at any time, turn my back towards you during the supposed confrontation, wouldn't it have been more natural for you to hit me on the face, the side or top of the head rather than *directly* on the back?
Police:	But –
Myself:	Would you please give me a straight answer yes or no.
Police:	W-well, yes.
Myself:	The truth is, you three approached me, asked for a light and for no reason whatever started to kick me on the stomach and groin. And when I tried to fight back I was arrested and dragged to the police station where I became aware for the first time that you were police officers. And while sitting quietly on a bench with my head resting on my

|||hands, waiting for the charge you were going to prefer, it was then that one of you wilfully gave me a severe blow on the back of the head with a truncheon. Is this not the honest truth?

Police: No.

I looked at the judge: 'That is all, my lord.' I had heard him addressed by that title. And as I had no experience in legal proceedings I hoped he would take pity on me – especially since I felt he would see through the lying police officers whom I thought were rather stupid in that they had evidently expected me to be cowed and speak incoherently. This was plain from the surprise on the face of each man under my cross examination during which the judge had put in a question or two to them and me. While I answered mine without hesitation they had to grope for words. I had asked a lot more questions during the cross examination, which I haven't mentioned here.

I was then asked to go to the witness box to give my version.

And soon I was addressing the court: I told of the incidents in the 1919 race riot, my services in the army and mercantile marine, why I left England and why I came back. I gave the reason for my buying the gun, which I pointed out to be brand new and not defective in any way; there was no question about that, neither was there any question of it being jammed – it was a revolver and not an automatic pistol which was far more likely to jam. I pointed out that its five chambers were fully loaded and added:

'If one bullet had failed to explode as the police want you to believe what was to prevent me pulling the trigger the second time before I was overpowered when, according to their own statement and the offence of which I am charged and now facing before the court, I was attempting to commit a murder? If I had the gun in my hand when being questioned, jumped three paces backward and fired a shot at the same time, as the police want you to believe, then failure to pull the trigger more than once when I had the initial advantage couldn't have been due to slowness on the draw, for according to the police, I had the gun in my hand even before I was questioned.'

I pointed to the position of the wound on my head and said, 'In my opinion, it is not only a physical impossibility, but quite an unnatural action for an opponent facing a desperate gunman with a loaded gun levelled at him, to walk or even jump round the gunman and strike a blow at the back of his head.'

I finished by saying that there wasn't an iota of truth in the whole of the police statement, that the whole story was nothing but fabrication based on hatred and colour prejudice.

The judge then began his summing up. By the time he was through, one of my guards nudged me and whispered, ' Darkie, I think you're going to get off.'

He was right. It has been a long time since, but if I remember rightly, I don't think the jury left their seats. The verdict was not guilty.

As I was walking out of the building, two old ladies stopped me in the hall. They both patted me on the back and said ' God bless you, son.' One of them stuffed £5 in my pocket and said ' Keep this, son, it may come in handy till you get a job.' Even though I protested that I had money, she wouldn't take it back.

Those two old ladies were white, and this I thought was remarkable. The hatred I had harboured towards all whites during my month's detention awaiting trial had disappeared completely.

One thing is certain: I have made England my home and intend to live here for the rest of my life. Why? Because in a British court of law there is no prejudice. Regardless of race, colour, religion or nationality a person is innocent until proved guilty, and a fair trial is given to all. Of course, there have been miscarriages of justice even in Britain, but only when there has been overwhelming evidence against the accused, due either to fabrication or some very unusual circumstances pointing to guilt.

Being a socialist at heart, even as a child, I have always had the desire to know others, to understand them, to respect their point of view – even if I do not agree. And most of all I have a strong sense of justice; for this reason I have always looked an aggressor in the eye and defied him to do his worst.

4
RETURN TO AMERICA

Three years after my acquittal at the Liverpool Assizes and after many voyages as ship's steward, without getting involved in any trouble, I decided to leave Liverpool and try my luck in Manchester. Though I had not been attacked since my acquittal I always had a feeling of apprehension walking the Liverpool streets.

Besides, I was informed that Manchester was liberal, the distance wasn't far and the fare was cheap; though I had saved some money from my last ships and wasn't exactly broke I wanted my money to last as long as possible.

I took my new-found friend, Charlie, along with me. Without first looking for digs we booked our cases in the station and went straight down to the shipping office at Salford and the docks, hunting for a ship. And because we were lucky we found one the same day, the ss *Manchester Corporation*, one of the Manchester liners, sailing to Canada. We signed on as stokers, made the trip and back.

By this time I had started drinking in public houses as a social pastime; in those days it was the only pleasure for coloured men, apart from going to the pictures or playing card games. There were the dance halls but very few of them would allow coloured people in. Even if they did, there was no one to dance with, for no white girl would dance with a black man and negresses were few and far between. Sometimes fights took place between whites and blacks as sexual jealousy flared. So we were left with the pubs.

On the day we were paid off the *Manchester Corporation*, Charlie and I decided to go to the Bull's Head at Greengate, Salford, for a good time. This was a well-known public house where most coloured people met, in fact there were usually more coloured people there than white. No sooner had we jumped off the tram a couple of blocks from the pub when we encountered a drunken mob. As soon as they saw our black faces, they pounced on us.

We were saved by the police through the screaming women, who tried to stop their men from their savage action. But the beating cost me my job, for I was still unfit to sign on my ship the following week for the next voyage.

It was after this occasion that I obtained my second revolver, a .38 Smith & Wesson. I bought it from another seaman one morning at the docks while out looking for a ship soon after my recovery from the attack; my sole intention was to use it the next time I was attacked by any mob or even by an individual bigger than I. By this time I had begun to hate with intensity any kind of injustice, and was determined to repulse it, whatever the cost, if I ever encountered it again.

After a few weeks of hunting the docks and shipping offices, I signed on the ss *Manchester Shipper* sailing to Canada and the USA. There was a sea bully on the ship called Jim Boyd. This man loved to play poker but he couldn't stand losing. Whenever he lost he would pick a row with the winner and grab back his money on some pretence or other; he always got away with it for no one dared to argue with him. I always tried to avoid playing in any game he was in, for I'd made up my mind that if he ever tried it on with me he would never get away with it. And naturally I wanted to avoid trouble. But I soon realized that avoiding trouble was an impossibility.

As we were playing draw poker in the foc'sle one evening in mid-Atlantic on the way to St John, New Brunswick, Jim left his own poker school and came and joined the one I was in. One look at him and I made a move to leave, then I decided otherwise. Why should I please him?

After a while Jim and I clashed on a hand. I had gone in with two aces, drew three cards and made four aces. It happened Jim had four kings after having drawn two cards. Not often two good hands like this come out in a deal so Jim naturally thought he had the better hand, especially after having seen me draw three cards. After raising and back-raising each other, Jim finally called with a wide grin spreading his cards on the table: 'Four kings; lemme see you beat that.'

'Four aces,' I said calmly and spread out my hand. And as I drew the pool I knew what was going to happen.

Jim's grin had disappeared. Now his face was grim and ugly, his eyes full of hate. He knocked my hands off the money. 'Take your bloody hands off that money befo' I knock your bleedin' 'ead off,' he growled. Then he began to draw the money to himself with a fierce look. 'You think I didn't see you slip them aces from your sleeve? You picked on the wrong one this time, you thieving little bastard!' Stuffing the money into his dungaree pocket, he glared at me. 'And one word from you, I'll wring your stinking neck . . .'

I took his advice and never said a word. He was a big six-footer and powerful. I walked calmly away from the table, took out the remaining few shillings I had left in my pocket, moved towards my bunk and pretended to put it into my sea bag, which I often used as a pillow. As I went into the bag I left the money and grabbed hold of my gun, which was already loaded. I pulled it out, slipped it under the bag and put my finger on the trigger. There was an old American proverb: 'Smith and Wesson makes all men equal.' But there was a big difference – I was more equal. I turned to face him.

'You bloody uncouth bastard! The liberties you have been taking in this ship have come to an end. And if you don't put every penny of my money on that bloody table right now, you're going to be very sorry.'

He was so surprised at being spoken to like this, and by a little man like me, that for a moment he was speechless. He looked at me as if he couldn't believe his own ears. Then all hell broke loose. He rushed at me like a bull in a china shop, snorting like a horse, pushing down everybody in front of him and uttering profane oaths. A moment later he stopped dead in his tracks when he saw the muzzle of a .38 Smith & Wesson pointing straight at him; there was an explosion as I pulled the trigger and a bullet whizzed past him and hit the bulkhead.

He came back to life suddenly and rushed straight for the nearest porthole, the door not being nearby. He seemed to lose all sense of reason and tried to push himself through the porthole and dive overboard, which would have meant certain death anyway had he succeeded. The task, however, was absolutely impossible for a big broad-shouldered man like Jim; all he could get through was his head.

I didn't mean to kill him. However, I would have been compelled to do so through fear had he made another move towards me after the warning shot. But luckily for him, and perhaps me, he took another course. All I really wanted to do was to give him the scare of his life, get back my money and check his damned bullying once and for all. These I achieved. For though I did not know it then, this was the end of Jim's bullying.

I took aim, pulled the trigger once more and sent a bullet crashing near the porthole about ten inches away from him; I watched him shaking with fear. The rest of the men had by this time scampered under the bunks. When I ordered him to face me he withdrew his head and prostrated himself before me, begging and whimpering for his life and making wild promises.

Now that I was master I don't mind admitting I felt great. A great big fifteen-stone bully lying prostrate before me, begging for his life and promising to be my slave for the rest of the trip was something out of this world. I couldn't believe it. From now on, I thought, no one was going to catch me without a gun. It was my turn to lay down the law and that I certainly did.

I thought it was time he knew other people had their rights. To make this sink in so that he would never, never forget, I fired another shot over him. He suppressed a scream and trembled with terror. I then gave him a short lecture about moral principles and brotherliness which, by his vigorous nodding, he accepted with alacrity. Then I ordered him to rise slowly and face me, and warned that any sudden move from him would also mean sudden departure from this earth. I knew he was too scared to do anything by then, but I felt good giving *him* the orders.

While Jim was obeying my orders and emptying his pockets

to return my money, news had reached the bridge that there was gun-shooting in the foc'sle. The door opened and in came the Old Man and the mate.

I was asked to hand over the gun. I refused to do so, but suggested going up to the bridge with them if I was accompanied by one of the stokers, for I had something to say and needed a witness. The captain agreed and the four of us went up to the bridge. Jim was glad to stay behind, but was told that he would be sent for if required. I picked up every penny before I left.

The Old Man was then told the true nature of the case and the disposition of Jim Boyd. My statement was backed by the stoker. I handed over the gun, but not before the captain promised not to let Jim know that I had done this. The stoker agreed with me. I could trust him not to tell for none of them liked Jim: they were simply afraid of him.

The captain then sent for Jim and told him that I had refused to surrender the gun but that I had promised not to interfere with him again if he in turn promised not to interfere with me. Jim fell on his knees before the Old Man and swore by all the gods that he'd never interfere with me again; he was very sorry for the whole matter, and that it was only a question of misunderstanding.

Damn right it was, I thought, it took Smith & Wesson to make him understand. The Old Man made us shake hands.

And Jim kept his promise. In fact he became good for the rest of his life. He died in the beginning of 1970, forty-four years later.

But though Jim had become humble and seemed to have accepted the doctrine of brotherly love, I had such a feeling of apprehension all the way to St John that I could hardly sleep or walk about without looking over my shoulder. By the time we arrived at Philadelphia I was nearly a nervous wreck. I jumped the ship there, for apart from the fact that Jim was keeping to his promises too well for my peace of mind, I suspected I might face a charge when we arrived back in England.

I became friendly with an Americanized Jamaican professional gambler by the name of McClean: we shared a flat and I teamed up with him. We did well for a time, but then luck turned against us and we had to go out labouring to pick up stakes, only to lose the lot again. I was frustrated and thought the life was too unsettled, so I decided to quit and find me a ship.

After roaming round the waterfront for a while I found a job on a coaster, the ss *Flagg* of the Southern Steamship Lines, sailing between Pennsylvania and Texas. As the ship was still in port I was acting as a port donkeyman on an eight-hour watch – from midnight to 8 am. One evening while gambling ashore McClean and I got broke in a crap game and I had to pawn my new gun to the croupier (my old gun had of course not been given back to me by the captain on the *Manchester Shipper*). As it was nearly time for me to get back aboard to do my watch I gave McClean the money and asked him to come along to my ship so that he could hustle with it if there was a game going on on board, which would leave me without interference to go below and do my watch.

This was 11.30 pm. Going to the ship we had to pass through 2nd Street on to the waterfront and then to the pier. 2nd Street was a kind of meeting place for most of the young Irish when they wanted to make whoopee at night. It was also a dangerous quarter between the hours of 10 pm and midnight, for most of them were about drunk then.

It is no secret that when the Irishman has had one over the eight there is nothing he likes more than a lovely good fight and that was one thing I didn't want to get mixed up in for three reasons. First, I wasn't supposed to be in the USA; I had entered illegally. Secondly, I didn't want to take any risk as I was in no position to fight a mob without a gun. And thirdly, in more amusing vein, I had a corn on my foot which was really painful. I was limping all the way and was therefore in no condition to run in case of an attack.

McClean was a very boastful fellow, and always inclined to raise his voice when speaking. To be on the safe side, as we walked along 2nd Street, I said to him,

'Boy, take it easy, it's kind o'late and these guys around here are kind o'tough and dangerous at this time of night.'

He retorted, 'Wha' you mean take it easy, this is a free country, ain't it?' and he became even louder. 'And wha' you mean dangerous? Look here, Markie, there ain't no man badder than me in this part of Philadelphia.'

'I ain't denying you, boy,' I said lamely, 'but right now I ain't taking no chances. I ain't got no gun and I can't run.'

'So what!' roared McClean, 'you's in good company, ain't you? I've my Betsy right here.' He touched his breast pocket to reassure me and continued: 'Ama tell you, there ain't no man in South Phili who could use this baby like me; so stop worrying, will you?'

'I ain't exactly worrying, McClean,' I moaned, 'but you talk so loud and I don't want no trouble, that's all. Just take it easy.'

But McClean just wouldn't have any of it. The more I tried to keep him quiet the louder he got. He began to tell me how once, before I came to Philadelphia, he had a fight with an Irish mob; he slashed down ten of them with his 'Betsy' and the rest had to run like hares.

I wasn't feeling happy at all. There were drunks all over the street; it only required one of them to start something and we would be bang in trouble.

As these thoughts were racing through my mind, a drunk staggered by and accidentally bumped into McClean.

McClean turned round and grabbed hold of the man by the lapel, shook him and growled, 'Why the hell don't you goddamn well look where you going?'

McClean was loud, but this drunk was ten times louder. 'Wha' the hell do you mean pushing me about? You goddamn black bastard!' he trumpeted.

Just around the corner under a lamp-post was a gang of young Irish, drinking moonshine and making whoopee. I tried to pacify the two, but the more I tried the louder they got. We were spotted and all hell broke loose.

Before I could pull myself together McClean was hitting the trail with more speed than a Derby winner.

It was a miracle how my corn suddenly disappeared. A genuine miracle! Before the first man could lay his paws on me I was off like a flash, right behind McClean. The chase began. And while trying to lengthen the distance between myself and the mob, I was not thinking especially kind thoughts about McClean.

I looked back. The crowd was getting bigger and I heard a shot. I've always had long legs and I opened up. In no time I'd reached and passed McClean. I heard another shot and ran even faster. After a few minutes of this supersonic speed I plucked up enough courage to look back to see how things were shaping. To my surprise and peace of mind I saw only one man behind me. A few yards ahead of me was the pier, my ship and safety. I waited for him. And as he reached to grab me I gave him a stiff upper-cut which landed nice and square, took him off his balance and knocked him down. I told him to get up and added, ' Now that's only two of us left, it's either you or me.'

The idiot was so intent on beating up a nigger, he didn't know that all his buddies had given up the chase. He got up and looked back. Seeing no one behind him he turned and fled like a hare. To speed him up I stamped my feet on the ground as if I was chasing him. He doubled up so much speed one would think he was a greyhound.

McClean was not so fortunate: after the second shot he decided to take a turning which turned out to be a cul-de-sac and was cornered by the mob. He wasn't killed but he was left as good as dead, and lucky at that for he was saved in the nick of time by a squad of police officers who were either going on or off duty when they heard the shots and ran to the spot with drawn pistols.

I paid him a visit at the hospital a few days later and couldn't recognize him from a mummy. I asked him what happened to his Betsy. He made no reply.

I wasn't sorry for him, he looked for it and got it, but he had nearly got me into it too.

I was in troubled waters wherever I went. I just couldn't get away from it. And so I came to find myself an enemy of the chief oiler on the *Flagg*, a Texas negro. At first I couldn't understand why he harboured this ill-feeling towards me, but I soon realized. It was because this man, who had been on the ship longer than anyone else, considered himself to be the head man. Any stoker or oiler who wanted a job on this ship should first see him. In my ignorance I had applied directly to the first assistant engineer, who is equivalent to the second engineer on a British ship (the second engineer on a British ship usually employs the engine-room staff).

A few nights after the 2nd Street incident I was ten minutes late getting aboard. As I arrived down below to take over the watch I saw a strange man on the job. Wondering what was happening, I asked him what he was doing there. He replied that he was the new twelve to eight donkeyman. If I'd been fired I knew nothing about it. I asked him who employed him and he said it was the chief oiler. I told him that I was the official donkeyman and ordered him out of the engine room. After a lot of argument he left.

As I was coming out of the bath the next morning after my watch I was told that I was wanted by the first assistant. I dressed quickly. When I reached his cabin the chief oiler was there obviously making a complaint.

The engineer asked me if I was late on my last watch. I replied, ' Yes, but only ten minutes, and it won't happen again.'

' But that wasn't the first time,' he said.

' But it was,' I said, ' in fact I am usually ready to take over by eleven-fifty.'

He glanced at the chief oiler and then looked at me and said, ' Okay, but don't let it happen again, not even for a minute.'

' Thank you, sir,' I replied.

No sooner had I got on deck when the oiler approached me with a gleam in his eye, pointing a threatening finger. ' You goddamn li'l bastard! Ama beat the daylight out o' you right now!' Immediately he threw a punch at me and followed up with many more which took me off balance. And as I fell he kicked me.

Never in my life have I weighed any more than nine stone. I was certainly no match for him and I knew it, for he was about fourteen stone, with a wonderful physique to match. To make matters worse, the ropes and wires on deck weren't helping me any. I kept tripping over them as he punched me. The bo'sun and some of the stevedores tried to stop him, for they could see that it was an uneven fight. But he didn't want to know. Blood was trickling down all over my face but somehow I couldn't feel the punches. Perhaps I was too infuriated to feel anything.

Finally he was stopped. By this time I was bruised all over, blood flowing from my nose and my silk shirt torn to ribbons. I've always had a vicious temper when aroused, now I was like a madman. If my gun hadn't been pawned I might have shot him dead on the spot.

Nevertheless I challenged him to come off the ship on to the pier shed and he promptly accepted. The bo'sun tried to stop him for he didn't think I'd have a chance, but I insisted. I thought if I could get him on the pier shed, where I could run around without being tripped by wires and ropes I stood a good chance. I was twenty-four and twelve years younger than he. And I was almost certain that my boxing experience would be an advantage; besides, I used to train in gymnasiums at least twice a week up to the time I joined the ship.

With plenty of room I was almost certain I could ride most of his punches until he got tired. I was equally certain he would tire sooner than me – if only I could save myself from being knocked out before then. Anyway, I thought, if he couldn't knock me unconscious after all the blows he'd given me, with all those bulging muscles, he couldn't be much good for a heavyweight.

We went on to the pier followed by a gang of excited stevedores and sailors. I took off what remained of my shirt. He was in his BVD (sleeveless underwear).

The biggest and toughest fist fight I'd ever had in my life began. The fight lasted about half an hour non-stop. I had a lot of encouragement from the onlookers. My face was not pleasant to look at and my body was smeared with my own blood, yet I refused to allow the fight to be stopped. I knew that time was in my favour and was determined to stay the course.

Eventually he was puffing and blowing like a windbag. He began to ask if I hadn't had enough; but I took no notice and kept on hitting, dancing away and riding his wild punches. Finally I saw my opening. I stepped in quickly, grabbed hold of the front of his BVD with my left hand, and with my right hand behind his neck, pulled him towards me; with all my weight and the last ounce of my strength I jumped up and butted him square on the nose.

His first blood began to spout from his nose like a fountain.

As he raised his hands to protect it I gave him a tremendous dig in the stomach with my knee and followed up with some rapid kidney punches. He squealed like a pig, begging me to stop, whimpering repeatedly that he'd had enough.

I have yet to meet a bully who can take his own medicine. I had taken his beatings for nearly three-quarters of an hour and yet he couldn't take one minute of mine.

To my surprise the first assistant engineer, who had witnessed the fight, fired him on the spot.

Walking along the waterfront on my way home one morning after doing my watch and soon after the fight with the Texan, my face still swollen, I noticed a crowd of negroes on a corner of the pavement, all kneeling. However they weren't kneeling to say their prayers: there was a crap game in progress and I decided to join in.

This was how my next trouble began. After watching the game for a few seconds, the next player picked up the dice. 'Two bucks I shoot,' he said and threw two dollars on the ground.

'You're covered,' I said and threw in my two dollars.

He rattled the dice and threw a ten. 'Big Dick from Boston,' he said fretfully. 'Who'll lay me two to one and say I don't make it?'

'I'll lay you five bucks to three you don't,' I answered.

'It's a bet,' he said mildly.

And as he went for his money to match my bet I saw him skilfully switch the dice. I pretended not to notice and allowed him to throw. As he did so, I went for the dice for I was certain he was playing with 'tops' (crooked dice) but I had to have proof before I could make an accusation. He rushed to stop me but was too late; I'd already picked one up and that was enough.

As I was examining it, from the corner of my eye I saw his right hand moving towards his inside pocket. I rushed him immediately and gave him a good butt in the stomach, at the same time grabbing hold of his hand to stop him getting the gun he was obviously reaching for. We both fell on the ground, but I was on top pelting him as hard as I could. He was about my size, which made my task easier.

I wrenched the gun away and ordered him to stay put while I closely examined the dice. As I'd expected, they were tops. By this time someone had snatched the pool money from the ground but it didn't make any difference to me because I confiscated ten bucks of his own money, which made me richer by an extra three bucks for my trouble. I also walked away with his revolver.

All this happened in less than three minutes. When I walked away the pavement was crowded with pedestrians, all looking on, but no one stopped me.

News travels fast on the waterfront and in no time people began to look up to me. But the name I was creating for myself wasn't of my own making. I began to hear remarks like these: 'You can't fool around with him, he's wild . . . where he comes from, folks eat folks.'

I didn't mind all the remarks because it kept the tearaways from me. In fact, once I overheard one coloured fellow say to another, 'You see that bozo over there, keep away from him – he's worse than a Red Indian! He comes from Africa; they don't scalp you over there, man, they just put you in the pot!'

A few days after the dice game on the street corner I was sitting in a snack bar between South and Broad Street, having something to eat when someone tapped me on the shoulder. Looking round I saw the face of the ugliest and toughest-looking negro I had ever seen. He had the trade mark of a prizefighter, a broken nose and cauliflower ears to match.

He was grinning at me. 'You's the African guy who beat up the big bozo at the pier a week ago, uh?'

In a broken voice I asked him what he wanted.

'You's the craziest bozo I ever did see,' he said with a cynical grin. 'Then you go an' pick a row with Alec an' take his rod away. H'mm, if that ain't crazy, nothing else is!'

'What do you want?' I repeated, half in fear, half in anger.

He took a deep breath. 'Whatever you is, man, you's the only one of its kind. An' talk 'bout luck, oh brother! That was Alec the Smoke whose rod you took away. Man, you'll live to be a hundred.' He snorted. 'Montana wanna see you anyway.'

'Who's Montana?' I asked, my lips quivering.

He became aggressive and more ugly. 'Say,' he growled, 'you ain't figuring on giving me no trouble, is you? Wha' you mean, who's Montana? Don't get smart, boy, don't get smart!' He paused and peered at me, brow wrinkled. 'Maybe you don't even wanna live to see tomorrow.' He barked, 'Look, boy, there's only one Montana in South Phili and that's Joe Montana. An' when Montana wanna see somebody, he see somebody! C'mon don't gie me no trouble now, is you coming or is you ain't?'

I looked around; there wasn't a friendly face in sight. There didn't seem to be much choice.

He had a car outside and made me sit in the front with him. I had heard of Montana Joe before, though I did not know which Montana he had meant; nearly everybody in South Philadelphia had heard of him. But I had never met him. Maybe it was curiosity, maybe it was fear, but I knew better than to cause any trouble.

We drove through South Street, going towards the waterfront, and then turned right at 7th Street. The car stopped right in front of a pool room.

'Okay, buddy, that's it.'

We walked into the pool room. My guard then guided me into a far corner of the room and gave me a chair.

'Wait here,' he said, smiling, 'and don't worry, 'cause there ain't nothing to worry 'bout. The boss is busy right now but ama get you a cold drink.' He sauntered to the bar.

The room was rather smoky, which wasn't surprising since all the tables were occupied. At one were two well-dressed and important-looking men; stuck between their teeth were fat expensive-looking cigars which looked to me like Elproductors. One was a fat coloured man with piggish eyes, the other was lanky and looked white, but after a second glance could have been white or coloured.

After a while the fat man went out and the slim man went through a door into another compartment. My guard then tapped me on the shoulder. 'C'mon, let's go.' He took me through this door which opened to a passage. At the end of the passage there was another door. He knocked at it and a voice said, 'Okay.'

We walked into a well-furnished office. Sitting behind the only table in the room was the slim man. He looked up from what he was doing and said with a smile, ' Sit down.'

He seemed to be expecting me. He came straight to the point. ' So you are a seaman on a coaster. What do they pay you?' he asked haughtily.

' Ninety bucks a month plus,' I answered fretfully.

' That's chicken feed,' he croaked with a flourish and went on, ' I've been looking for a good man, a guy who can fight without a rod, a guy who ain't yeller, to replace one of my men who got buried last week.'

' Replacing buried men isn't one of my hobbies,' I said uneasily.

He laughed aloud and looked towards ' Zombie ' who was standing behind me.

' Hey, Butch, this boy got sense o' 'umour.' He looked back at me and continued, ' I control all of these territories south of Gerrard Avenue. There's plenty of hoodlums I could choose from but I don't wan'em, you know why? If they have a rod they start shooting at their own shadows, if they ain't got no rod they'se yeller as ripe bananas. I don't like my men carrying rod, that way they can't shoot a cop when cornered. I've been on this racket ever since the beginning of prohibition and I ain't never got no trouble with the cops; that way I operate. I pay all mouthpiece and fines; Butch will show you round and tell you what to do. That's all.'

Before I could resent or even make up my mind I found myself following Zombie out of the office into the pool room. As we came to the pool room, he whispered, ' There's a big party going on in Bainbridge Street, that's one of my rounds. C'mon, meet some of the broads.'

Entering the car he smiled winningly at me. ' You know sump'n, you's a lucky guy. Montana is mighty careful who he choose.' He added seriously, ' Ama tell you sump'n else too, ain't nobody in the State of Pennsylvania as swell as Montana, nobody.'

Up to then I didn't exactly know what kind of a job it was but I had a good idea. This was 1926. Prohibition was in effect, the Charleston was the craze, wild drinking parties and speakeasies were the vogue. Big names like Bugs Moran and Al

Capone were on the lips of everyone. It could mean only one thing: liquor. And this could be dangerous.

I found Zombie to be quite talkative. He kept me busy trying to think and listen to him at the same time.

He pulled the brake suddenly, rubbed his hands together and grinned broadly, 'That's it, buddy, let's go to town.'

We walked up a flight of stairs and stopped in front of a door. We could hear the sound of a piano playing and the sound of laughing voices. He knocked once, paused, and knocked again.

As the door opened, I saw the most exciting creation of the feminine gender I had ever encountered. Her skin was brown and soft, flashing big brown eyes, jet black glossy hair well placed, and her figure was next to none. I thought if ever a woman was created – she was!

She smiled at us, showing a perfect set of teeth that glittered like pearls. With a sexy, soft, husky voice, she said, 'Hello, Butch, please do come in.'

She stood aside to let us pass. As I passed I looked back at her, our eyes met. Immediately I fell in love with her with every fibre of my being. It was right there and then I decided to join Montana's organization. I followed Butch into a large well-furnished room. Couples were dancing the Charleston to the tune of 'I wonder where my baby is tonight' which was being played on a piano in a corner of the room by a young well-groomed man. In the opposite corner was a victrola (cabinet gramophone). Those not dancing were sitting around chatting happily and holding on to their glasses of 'john steady' (illicit liquor).

Just then the music stopped. Butch began to give me an introduction:

'Well fellers and broads, I wan' you all to meet Markie; he's a buddy of Montana and a mighty swell guy too; you gonna see a lot o' him from now on.'

I waved my hands and said 'Hello,' but all the time my mind was on this fabulous woman. I looked back towards the door and there she was, standing in the hallway with a man who was busy doing a lot of talking but to whom she didn't seem to be paying much attention. Our eyes met once more, my heart missed a beat.

She left the fellow standing by himself and came up to me. 'Hello,' she said with the same soft husky voice, 'I'm Viola, I don't think I remember seeing you before.'

I smiled. 'What have we both been missing?' I asked.

Just then the pianist started playing one of Bessie Smith's blues. I put my hand around her waist. 'Let's dance,' I said, and held her close to me.

That's how I met Viola. This glorious divinity was going to cause me a lot of trouble, yes, a lot of trouble! But at that moment I was in heaven.

Butch, as I must now call Zombie, turned out to be a very pleasant and entertaining person. I could hardly believe he was the same man whose zombie-looking face was leering at me not too long ago. I had a wonderful time. I didn't dance with anyone else except Viola, to the annoyance of the man who was talking to her before she came to me. If black looks could kill I would have been completely annihilated.

I suddenly realized that it had gone 11.30 pm and I had to go to work. After all, I was still employed aboard the ss *Flagg*.

One thing I'd never done in my life was to let anybody down. I had already made up my mind that under no circumstances would I sail on the *Flagg*, not after seeing and meeting this gorgeous beauty. No matter how dangerous Montana's job was going to be, I couldn't give a damn. With Viola around I felt I could face Lucifer himself and tell him where to get off.

It was only a few hours since Butch's ugly face had leered at me in the snack bar. Now it seemed as if I'd known him all my life. But I had to go back on the ship, do my watch and give my notice to the first assistant so he could get someone else in my place. I arranged a date with Viola and told Butch what I had to do.

'Man, you can't do that,' he snarled. 'You's working for Montana now, and nobody makes a monkey out o' Montana.'

He was half soused with liquor and looked very ugly. But after I'd explained everything he took it well and offered to drive me down to the pier.

After I came to know Montana I found him to be a 'swell guy' as Butch had said. Butch and I worked the same rounds. Our job was to deliver liquor, every two men to an allotment.

If there was any slackness of orders from any particular quarter it was also up to us to find out why. We didn't bully or manhandle anybody: Montana didn't like it that way. We used psychology. Sometimes we met people who didn't want to understand psychology. To these people we used other methods, such as convincing them that our brand of liquor was more mature and contained no poisoning ingredients like the others. This always worked when added with a slight threat. We never had any serious trouble – not even with the police. Perhaps they knew we were not hoodlums, at least not the kind one would expect in that business.

Our clients wanted our liquor just as much as we wanted their money. We sold good liquor, not the kind that is made and sold the same day. I'd drunk some of this at some of the parties I'd cause to attend.

What I could never understand up to now was why they ever made the prohibition law at all. There were more people drinking hard liquor in prohibition days than there were in the whole history of the United States of America. People always clamour for the forbidden fruits. Liquor was made for those who like it and many do; many of those who don't, take it occasionally if it's just to make merry at special events. And even the New Testament tells us that wine was multiplied by Our Lord at a wedding.

When the state or government, by imposing such ridiculous laws, tries to prevent the individual doing what comes naturally, they not only encourage people to break the law but they also incite corruption. Restricted laws in cases like this could be tolerated. But certainly not prohibition. Drinking is a right of all men. During the days of prohibition in the USA, thousands of lives were lost, killed by bootleg liquor and gangsterism because of the ridiculous law.

I didn't remain long in the racket. I left it, not because I repented my evil ways, which were making me easy money and satisfying everyone all round, but for another, more sinister reason.

One evening, while standing on the corner of 5th Street and Passyunk Avenue, all pleased with myself, a big 'Philadelphia hand-made' cigar stuck in my mouth, and thinking of the Dempsey v Tunney world heavyweight fight due shortly which was the topic of the day, a big car suddenly stopped in front of me. And before I knew what was happening I was thrown into it and hit on the back of the neck, which nearly made the cigar get jammed in my throat. And then my gun was taken away. There were three men in the car, one of uncertain origin, two coloured. After driving for about twenty minutes the car stopped in front of a house and I was hustled in and into a large room.

One of the negroes barked, ' Who you working for?'

Because I was too dazed to answer since it had all happened so suddenly, he walked up and gave me a stinging blow on the jaw. ' H'mm, you won't talk, eh? Who you working for I say?'

And now that I had come to realize they were bootleggers from another gang, I answered meekly, ' I'm working for myself.'

' Okay, wise guy, how je like to get taken for a ride?' commented the one of uncertain origin, walking towards me menacingly. He glared at me and then followed up by giving me a stinging blow on the temple, which knocked me down but not out.

Thinking I was unconscious, they lifted me up and carried me out of the room. I thought they were really taking me out for a ride so I feigned complete unconsciousness. Instead I was taken down to a basement, dumped in the middle of the room and left alone with one of the negroes. I noticed the man had a holster as he took his jacket off, the basement being hot. He sat down in the far corner, rolled a cigarette and lit it.

I lay down there thinking of all sorts of ways to get out of this. Just then the other negro walked in and muttered something to the other fellow. They both walked towards me. I was shaking with fright, and yet I didn't think they were going to kill me there for I couldn't see any sense in that. The newcomer turned me over with his foot and roared, ' You ready to talk? You better be for we ain't got no time to waste with you.'

' W-what do you want of me?' I stammered. ' I ain't done nothing to you, I don't even know you.'

' First, I wanna know who you working for,' he snarled.

' If you give me time and don't rush me I'll tell you everything,' I pleaded. ' I ain't got nothing to hide.'

' Okay, shoot!' he retorted.

'In the first place I told you the truth when I said I am working for myself,' I lied.

'Then where the hell you get your liquor from?' he demanded.

'I buy them from an Italian grocer by the gallon and sell them by the pint and half pint.' I added quickly, 'I can't give you the address 'cause I know the place only by sight. But I can take you there, it's somewhere around near the waterfront.' I hoped they would fall for this as it might give me the chance of attracting attention one way or the other on our way to the place. I sat up and looked at them pleadingly. 'I don't know what I've done to you or your friends but if I've done anything wrong I'm mighty sorry. I'm a stranger in this city . . .'

The third man then swaggered in, chewing a large cigar and running his eyes over me as I pleaded. 'Yeh! Come to think of it he sure talk funny,' he murmured after a moment. 'Where you come from?'

'Sierra Leone,' I answered, feeling relieved someone had noticed my accent.

He snapped, 'Sarah Lone! I don't wanna know who is your mother . . .'

'Sierra Leone,' I repeated. 'That's the name of the place I come from.'

'Ugh, what part of the States is that? Never heard of it.'

'It isn't in the States,' I said, 'it's in Africa, West Africa.'

One of the negroes yelled, 'Man, that guy is lying! He can't come from there, not if it's in Africa – that's a million miles from here!'

'Maybe he means Jewmaker,' said the other. 'That ain't no million miles from here.'

'He don't mean that,' snapped the cigar chewer. 'Jewmakans speak different. I've met plenty o' them.'

'Well, if he's really from Africa,' said the man who had accused me of lying, 'that's the first one I've seen. H'mm-h'mmm!'

'There's a couple o' them about,' the cigar chewer grunted. 'I met one the other day. Speaks just like him. He wasn't a bad feller.' Then he walked to the far corner of the cellar followed by the others. After a hurried consultation between them, which I supposed concerned my fate, they walked grimly towards me.

'We gonna turn you loose,' said the cigar-chewing man grimly. 'But if ever we see you snooping around anyway near our territory again, watch out!' Then he gave me back my gun minus the bullets.

The other two led me up the stairs, threw me in the car and drove off. It was now in the early hours of the morning. I recognized the names of one or two streets as we drove past, names which I was almost certain were in the German Town area. We drove for about half an hour without a word being spoken, and then stopped suddenly.

'Get out,' growled the man sitting with me in the passenger seat. 'Consider yourself mighty lucky this time. You ain't gonna be that lucky next time.'

They drove off as suddenly as they had stopped.

I stood on the pavement, cold sweat running down me. For the first time in my life I was genuinely scared. I had no idea why they picked on me, for Butch and I had never delivered liquor in anybody else's territory. All our customers lived in the neighbourhood of South Street and all below Gerrard Avenue.

Perhaps it was a case of mistaken identity. But since I presumed their territory was in German Town and I had been at a party there on many occasions with Butch, perhaps they had felt we were in the business and thought we were trying to make contact. They never mentioned which their territory was and I was too frightened to ask questions.

I wandered about for some time trying to find out where they had dropped me and found I was somewhere in North Philadelphia. And since my money wasn't taken away my eyes roamed the deserted streets, looking for a taxi. I saw a lone yellow cab cruising and ordered it to take me to my flat in South Philadelphia.

It took me several minutes to get the key into the lock of my flat. I rushed in, opened a half pint of hooch and drank the lot. After my nerves were settled I lay down and began to think of my next move. What was I going to do? Should I quit? Should I tell Butch and Montana what had happened and carry on with the job?

I didn't sleep a wink. By nine in the morning I'd come to a decision. Why should I allow these two-bit hoodlums to scare me off a good living? I got up, doused my face with cold water and began to get ready to go to Butch's place so I could tell him all about it. But on second thoughts I decided not to tell him; I didn't want to get mixed up in any gang warfare, for I was sure that if Montana knew about it he'd probably know who the gang were and would retaliate. Anyway, I felt a lot better by this time. I undressed and went back to bed and had a good sleep.

A loud knock on the door woke me up. I looked at the clock on the dressing-table and found it had gone three. I put on my dressing-gown and opened the door. And there was Butch.

'Hey, wha' the hell's the matter with you? You don't look so good,' he croaked.

I grinned sheepishly. 'We-ll, I had a li'l bit too much last night and I'm sure feeling bad.'

'Been looking for you last night, couldn't find you – where you been, man?' he asked, lighting a cigar and eyeing me suspiciously.

'Oh, I-I went to German Town to see a friend.'

'Well, get dressed then, it's time we got moving,' he said in a flurry.

A month later I took Viola to the Standard Theatre on South Street to see Barlowe and Ashes, my then favourite coloured comedians. After the show we stood on the corner of 8th and South waiting for a cab. A car crawled by and I heard two shots fired, saw the car pick up speed and vanish round the corner.

When I looked around, a man was lying in a pool of blood on the pavement, holding on to his stomach. He had been shot. A minute before, that man had been standing just next to me.

I dropped Viola home, told her I wasn't feeling well and went home. I couldn't sleep all night for thinking of the hoodlums who had roughed me up. I just couldn't make myself believe that those bullets weren't meant for me.

The next morning I got myself a job on a coaster the ss *Grecian*, one of the Merchant and Miners Steamship Company, sailing to Savannah, Georgia, and Jacksonville, Florida. Later, in prison, news reached me that those bullets had been meant for me, just as I had suspected. But, ironically, they had nothing to do with the bootleggers who had roughed me. They were fired by one of Viola's drink-sodden, jealous ex-lovers. He wasn't sent to the chair (the man didn't die). But he was sent in for a long, long time.

5

IN AND OUT OF TROUBLE

My first taste of an American jail began one evening while my ship was lying alongside the pier at Savannah, Georgia. I was on my way back to the ship after a hectic time drinking corn liquor at Yamacrow, the coloured quarter. Walking unsteadily through the pier gate I said 'Hi!' to the gatekeeper, showed him my pass and brushed past. This, he thought, was insolent behaviour from a black man towards a white man. He grabbed me by the scruff, turned me round and slapped me hard on the face. 'You better learn some manners nigger,' he growled.

I was just about to retaliate when I noticed a few white men including two policemen, standing nearby, watching and grinning. I changed my mind. But he'd noticed my intention. He pulled his pistol and hit me violently on the head with it. For the very first time in my life I was afraid to hit back, and glad I had made it a policy never to carry an offensive weapon when on a drinking spree.

'Everyone of you goddamn northern niggers should be taught a lesson when you get down here,' he added with another slap. 'You dirty bastards!'

Had I lifted a finger to hit back I would have been shot dead right on the spot. No inquiry whatever! I wasn't too drunk to know this. I was in the deep South: he was white, I was black, that's all there was to it. After he'd had his sadistic pleasure he beckoned the grinning policemen. 'Lock him up.'

IN AND OUT OF TROUBLE

I was charged the next morning with being drunk and disorderly and insulting behaviour. I was fined thirty dollars or thirty days. By this time my ship had gone, so thirty days it was, for I had no more than two dollars on me.

The gaol wasn't like most gaols; it was in fact a police barracks somewhere in the city. The prisoners (all negroes) were left on their own and the only work was to brush down the police horses, polish the motor cycles and keep the place clean. There were also a few women prisoners to do the cooking and serve the meals. In the evenings we could gamble amongst ourselves as much as we liked without any interference from the guards.

After a few evenings of poker playing I won enough for the fine, which I paid to the warden and I was free. But unfortunately my freedom was short lived. I was arrested the same night.

It was in a gambling house in Yamacrow. The cops rushed the premises and started beating up every one of us. I made my first big mistake when I protested, a very silly thing for a negro to do. I at once became the centre of attraction and was beaten up mercilessly.

While crouching in the benchless cell the next morning, waiting to go before the judge, the cell door opened and in came a white man. After scrutinizing the lot of us, he asked, ' Any one of you guys want a mouthpiece?'

I nodded. ' Yeah, I can do with one.'

' I'm a lawyer,' he said, and swaggered towards me. ' How much dough you got?'

' About fifty bucks,' I said.

' You got it here?'

' Yeah, I got it here.'

' Now we can talk business,' he drawled.

Without asking me any details, he went on, ' You's in a mighty tough spot, boy; yaah, you sure is! But Ah reckon Ah may do sumpin' for you. Mind you, Ah ain't promising nothin', but Ah guess it can be arranged; wha's yore name?'

I told him.

' Okay, le's see the colour of yore money,' he said greedily.

After retaining five dollars out of fifty I gave him the rest. He began to leave hurriedly, but since he hadn't taken any particulars I shouted after him, 'Ain't you gonna ask me wha' happened?'

'Don't make no differen', boy, don't make no differen'.' Disappearing through the door, he added, 'Ah'll see you in court.'

I was finally hustled before Judge Swartz the same judge who had sent me in before. This judge was well-known in Savannah in the twenties.

The officer read the charge. As he began to elaborate my lawyer stood up and started to address the judge. 'Your Honour, this nigger...'

That was as far as he got for my forty-five dollars. The judge rapped his desk and snapped at him, 'Sit down!'

He sat down so quickly he nearly tumbled over.

I couldn't quite make out what the officer was saying as he gave 'evidence' because my head and ears were bandaged from the beating I'd received the night before; but when the judge looked at me and I saw his lips move I thought it was an invitation for me to speak on my own behalf. I began to tell my story. But before I had spoken two words I was hit on the back by the guard.

'Shurrup, nigger, while the judge speaks,' he snarled.

The judge didn't waste words, he simply sentenced me to ninety days in the Brown Farm prison.

This gaol was so-called because the prisoners wore brown uniform and the gaol was situated on a farm. There were only a handful of prisoners who actually worked in the prison itself and those were mainly trusties, some of whom did the farming, and some who did the cooking and served the meals. All the rest were taken out in trucks every morning, together with members of the notorious chain gang (transferred from Atlanta), heavily guarded, to work at another destination. The work consisted of digging ditches, cutting down trees and building bridges. Most of the work was done on swamps where sometimes the water was knee deep, sometimes higher. Most of the chain-gang prisoners were long-timers, some doing ninety-nine years and some even more. Why they had been given such long sentences was beyond my comprehension. I was one of the Brown Farm prisoners who worked with them. We were not secured with chains and were identified by our brown uniforms, while the chain-gang wore black-and-white stripes and each man was fettered with a heavy iron ball attached to the chain.

The guards were not issued with uniform and most appeared to be illiterate. But every one of them was a marksman. Most of them I think were hillbillies and hard-looking. I was told they could shoot and hit a silver dollar right in the centre in mid-air, but how true this was I cannot say. I often wondered why some of them had notches on the butts of their rifle and soon discovered.

While out at work digging trenches one day I overheard the following conversation between two guards.

'Say Bill, you ain't never tol' me wha' you got them fourth notch for.'

'Well, it happened thisaway,' said the other.' 'Ah was guarding some niggers way back in Tennessee when Ah 'appen to see one o' them made a dive. Boy, that sure was the la-as thing that nigger ever did! Ah bet 'e never even noo wha' 'it 'im. Ah got 'im right in the brain, yes sir! Right in the brain. Only one shot too.'

They both looked at me. One grinned cynically and the other simply spat a mouthful of tobacco juice at me.

In this prison we were up every morning at five o'clock, had a cold shower and then had breakfast, which usually consisted of cornmeal and coffee. We were then mustered in the yard to be checked, whites on one side, coloured on the other, the chain gangs with their chains and balls. After being checked we were ordered to get on the trucks. This was sometimes difficult for members of the chain gang, owing to their heavy fetters.

Guards were posted all round with rifles on the ready. We were then driven to our work which was usually ten or fifteen miles from the prison. Our lunch was carried with us, cornbread and pork. At 4 pm we would finish, get back on the trucks and return to the prison. Tea was served and then we were locked in, separately from the whites. While we were in we could smoke any brand of cigars we liked or read any kind of magazine, provided we had the money to pay for them. Money was seldom taken away from prisoners on reception in this prison as is the rule in all British prisons, provided of course the amount was not large. The privilege of selling any articles is usually accorded to lifers or long-term prisoners of good behaviour. Tobacco was given free by the prison authorities.

Some of the guards were kind while others were wicked and sadistic. The warden was as bad as the sadistic ones. Early one morning while on muster in the prison yard the warden was informed that a prisoner about to be released was a trusty and that another man was needed to replace him. The chief guard pointed in my direction. The warden then shouted at me to step forward.

To be a trusty was a position that most prisoners would jump at, but I wasn't interested. My only interest then was to finish my ninety days and get out of Georgia and anything that had to do with the South as fast as I could; furthermore, I wasn't quite sure whether the warden meant me or one of the men standing on either side of me, so I didn't step forward.

Thinking I was being insolent he stepped towards me and started whipping me with his cane.

'Nigger,' he snarled, 'when I say step forward I ain't meanin' nothin' else but!'

Because I didn't yelp or cry out he became angry. He rained his cane on me with temper. Then he ordered that I be put on the 'cooler' (a coop like a wardrobe with cold water dripping down).

A few days later while out working in the swamps with the chain-gang I heard a shot. Looking round I saw a chain-gang prisoner who had been working about two feet away from me lying stone dead with blood streaming from his temple. He was black. I'm not sure to this day why he was killed, one doesn't ask questions in such places. The general idea was that he was trying to escape. I just kept on doing what I was doing, only I did it much faster.

I left Georgia on the day I was released from prison. Not having any money for my fare to get out of the South, and not wishing to stick around waiting for a job on a ship, I stowed away on the first North-bound vessel, the ss *City of Columbus* of the Ocean Steam Ship Company, a large passenger-carrying coaster bound for Boston, Mass.

Strangely enough I was never discovered even though I didn't hide. I mixed freely with the crew, each department thinking I belonged to the next department. I was never short of food. And as dice and poker games were continually played amongst the crew, by the time we reached Boston I had multiplied the couple of dollars I had had when I boarded the ship to well over two hundred dollars. I stayed on the ship and played on for the couple of days she was lying at Boston. By the time she was ready to sail again I was the proud possessor of over a thousand dollars.

After she left I took a Pullman back to Philadelphia. I had sent Viola a telegram informing her I was coming and at what time I'd be arriving. She was waiting for me at the station.

We painted the town red the whole week. No matter what I spent the thousand dollars never seemed to get less. All I had to do after a hectic night was to go out and gamble some more and my roll would be as fat as ever. I just couldn't go wrong. For a whole month I had nothing but good luck – one of the few occasions when Old Man Trouble was busy somewhere else. Even Viola's jealous ex-lovers were too busy fighting amongst themselves to bother me. The only people who were bothering me were those who were eager to help me spend my winnings.

When a man has a big roll on him all the time, he always seems to have a lot of friends around him and that's how it was with me.

The idea struck me that if these people loved me so much why not make a racket out of them. And soon I was throwing weekend parties in my flat. Everybody got drunk free of charge on the first party. I then asked Viola to tell them that there was going to be a bigger party the following weekend and every weekend from then on. But what they weren't told was that they were going to pay for their liquor and they were going to buy it from me.

That was how I started my own racket. Everybody was invited and all who came were served with a plate of boiled pig entrails and cornbread and a small shot of 'whisky' – free.

After that lot, anybody who wanted some more 'whisky' had to pay for it. I charged twenty-five cents a shot. Every bottle I sold brought me ten bucks and I paid only a dollar a bottle. I sold about ten bottles a night. Now and then I'd give a free round but I'd get that back because nearly everybody would buy me a drink too. I didn't drink all they bought me but I charged them for it just the same. I gave Thelma, my pianist, ten bucks for the two nights in the week and as much drink as she wanted.

I could have had Thelma just for the drinks, but taking advantage of somebody's weakness has never been one of my principles. Thelma was the most talented pianist and vocalist I'd ever met, but liquor was her undoing. She'd play at any party for drinks rather than money provided she could drink as much as she wanted. And one didn't have to worry about her being too drunk to work; she could drink all day and night without being incapable. How she could accomplish such miraculous feats nobody knew.

I usually made about 160 bucks' clear profit every weekend. That way I didn't even have to gamble if I didn't want to, and no one could accuse me of muscling in on their territory. It also made me feel independent. I was working for nobody but myself. I made a party and they came, that's all there was to it. It was a success from the start. Viola would bring along a train of attractive ' broads ' to entice the suckers. And they would spend like millionaires.

I once heard a fellow say that many men will turn to look at a woman out of habit. But with Viola, when they turned to look they just stopped walking while they looked and that's not all. Viola could make a champion spendthrift out of a miser. The same fellows who used to hold on to their money while I spent mine were now practically throwing it at me, thanks to Viola and her friends.

All the same Viola brought danger with her. When I wasn't having trouble with some of her ex-lovers I would be arguing with her, especially when I paid extra attention to one or two of her girlfriends – and for this nobody could blame me, they were the most beautiful set of girls in one gathering – apart from a beauty contest. But Viola was possessive. And though possessive women were never my cup of tea, the more furious she was, the more crazy I seemed to get about her. And when she confronted me in temper, all I could see was her shapely bosom heaving up and down.

However as time went on I came to dislike her for her violent temper and my love began to decline. And even though I loved Philadelphia and had thought of going to the City Hall at Broad Street and applying for the necessary particulars to become an American citizen, with her increasing possessiveness and domineering attitude I began to wonder if it was worth it. She could be lovable one moment and horrible the next; and since she had been known to use the switch-blade she carried in her stocking, I came to consider her as dangerous.

On one occasion, during one of her violent fits, she attacked me with the knife. It was either her or me. I knocked her out with a piece of furniture. But not before some of the furniture had been smashed. I decided to put an end to our relationship. She did not approve of this and kept gate crashing my parties and causing trouble. And most of the time she'd be stinking drunk.

Since commonsense told me the law might turn a blind eye to the party racket but not to continual disturbances, I left the flat after making good the damage caused and moved to another. It had to be in South Phili, since that was the only part of town where I was known. But since I had to make parties for a living and had to spread the news of my whereabouts Viola had no trouble finding me. I kept moving, but no matter where I went she found me. She probably sensed I was afraid of her and was taking advantage of it.

There were only two things I could do: liquidate her or leave Philadelphia. I chose the latter and signed on a British ship, the ss *Manchester Merchant*. It was a very sad day for me as I stood on the deck, watching the only American city I'd ever loved pass by while sailing down the Delaware bound for Australia.

The *Manchester Merchant* was a very good ship, so was the Old Man, Captain J. H. Hudson. I stayed on it for about a year before being paid off at New York. But New York was no place for me, not since I was robbed of every penny I possessed within four hours of my arrival there, and though seven years had passed I still remembered the incident bitterly. In any case I would never have been paid off there if the ship hadn't renewed her charter for another Pacific run and wasn't expected back in England for another year. I never liked exceptionally long trips – especially if I had to go back on the same run.

As soon as I got paid off I took the first fast train to Philadelphia, hoping Viola had been bumped off or something. But no such luck. I hadn't been in the city twenty-four hours before I bumped into her. This called for an immediate exit. I couldn't find a ship quickly enough to get out, and since I didn't believe in paying fares on ships I stowed away on the first ship sailing for Britain, the ss *Manchester Corporation*, one of my old ships belonging to the same line as my last ship.

I was living like a lord among the stokers in the foc'sle, smoking big cigars and talking big, when someone squealed. So I was ' discovered ' and put to work. When the ship arrived in Manchester I was handed over to the police and sent before the magistrate. He couldn't make an order of deportation back to America because I was British. Instead he gave me a two weeks' prison sentence, which I served in Strangeways Jail.

When I came out I lived it up for a few weeks and became engaged to Alma, the mulatto girl I had been courting before I jumped the *Manchester Shipper* at Philadelphia. She was well brought up and nothing like Viola. But soon I was broke and had to go away again to find the money to get married. So I signed on the ss *Manchester Civilian* on 17 April 1928.

This was also a good ship with a good captain, Captain E. W. Raper. After eight months of coal trading along the Canadian coast we came back to Britain and got paid off at Falmouth on 7 December. By this time my fiancée was touring with Sir Alfred Butts's *Show Boat*. The banns were up before I arrived. She took a couple of days off from Edinburgh, came down to Manchester and we got married. She went back on tour and I signed on again on 18 December on the same ship bound for Brazil and Chile. After a few months spent trading round the South American coast we sailed from Junin, Chile, bound for New York via the Panama Canal.

Three days later, through force of circumstances, I was to become the leader of a protest march which nearly led to mutiny on the high seas.

The *Manchester Civilian* being a small cargo boat of about three thousand tons and not equipped with large cold storage, we could have fresh meat only for the first three days out of port, then followed by the regular preserved fare of tinned meat and salt beef. But on this occasion we were served with the preserved fare from the first day we left Junin. The men resented this strongly. And though it didn't matter to me one way or the other, I was going to be drawn into it. Ole Man Trouble saw to that.

After the third day when there was no change in the fare the men decided to march up to the bridge in protest. As it was out of the question for all of us to do so, a ballot was taken and it fell on the twelve to four watch, which was mine. The ship carried nine stokers (all negroes), three on a watch. It was decided that when the next watch was called at seven bells and the dinner was brought in for the relieving watch, which was mine, if the fare hadn't been changed we three stokers should go up to the bridge with the food and make a complaint to the Old Man.

I was chosen as the spokesman for I could express myself better than the other two. When the watch was called and dinner brought in, the food, as expected, was exactly the same. We three went up to the bridge carrying the food with us. But before we had time to see the Old Man, the chief officer, an habitual bully, came up aggressively and without listening to what we had to say, told us to leave the bridge before he had us thrown off.

At this stage I lost my temper and gave him a piece of my mind. The captain heard the row and came out of the chart room to see what it was all about, but by this time I was beyond control.

I threw the food overboard and went to the foc'sle and told the rest of the men to go on strike. But one of the men on the four to eight watch, more level-headed, said, 'It's dangerous to do that.'

Wide-eyed, he added, 'There'll be nothing to stop the captain sending a radio message, and before long the Royal Navy would be at us and we'd be in real trouble!'

I told him, in savage fury, that trouble was no stranger to me and a bit more of it would make no difference. But after the others had pleaded with me not to be rash, I relented. It was then that I suggested keeping the steam pressure at 150 pounds instead of the 190 which was the required pressure.

This would cause the ship to be at least three days late getting to New York, and a great financial loss to the company, which I thought would serve them right for employing a bully such as the chief mate, whom I had come to dislike intensely. And knowing she was on time charter I felt it would be an exact retribution. After pointing this out I added vehemently, 'And there's nothing they can do about it!' I went on to say that if we were prosecuted we could plead that we did our best and could do no more. To this all five men nodded vigorously. 'But,' I warned, 'we must under no circumstances keep the steam pressure less than 150; less than that would not be convincing if we were to be prosecuted, for any fool of a fireman should be able to do better. Okay?' All agreed.

When we three went below to relieve the eight to twelve watch, I told the three men on it all about the row and they in turn agreed.

So it was 150 pounds pressure. And my watch started it. By 1 pm the third engineer came into the stokehold and wanted to know what was wrong with the steam. We were stoking like mad in his presence. But it was the kind of nonsensical stoking that could never raise the steam any higher. Too much coal in the furnace and the fire not bright enough.

I turned to look at him. 'Don't ask us, you can see for yourself. Maybe the coal is bad.'

He watched us for some time and then went back into the engine room, shaking his head in despair. Like any marine engineer he knew we had no intention of raising the steam. He had run his eyes over the fire.

Soon, he was back with the chief engineer. The chief opened the furnace doors and one look at the black fires told him the kind of stoking we were doing. He told us not to be silly. We took no notice and kept pretending to be busy. A moment later both engineers left us without another word.

In nearly every merchant ship there is a 'sea-lawyer,' who knows all the answers until he comes face to face with authority; there were two of this kind on the second engineer's watch, the four to eight. With such men an engineer just had to show his face in the stokehold and they'd nearly blow up the boilers stoking up. And though we had all agreed on the steam pressure, I thought I would warn these two in no uncertain terms – especially since the rumpus was started by them in the first place.

About 3.40 pm, while the four to eight watch was getting ready in the foc'sle to relieve us, I did my last round, left the stokehold, went straight to the foc'sle and got my gun out. I began to clean it in front of the others. Each one of the stokers knew that I'd once been a gunman, but what they didn't know was that I had a gun aboard this ship. In their eyes I was a killer and I intended making use of this belief. The two sea-lawyers glanced apprehensively at the gun, which pleased me.

'Look here, fellers,' I said coldly, 'we are now keeping the steam to a hundred and fifty, no more, no less. But I'd like to make this point clear: now that we've started, we've got to see the end of it.' I looked hard at them. 'It's no use one watch keeping up to the rule if the others don't. From now on I'm gonna make it my business to sneak down below and see that every watch keeps to the rule.'

I passed my eyes from one to the other of the sea-lawyers and continued menacingly, 'And if I catch any watch breaking the rule I'll shoot down all three in the watch and won't care less what happens to me.' I paused. 'And if news reaches the Old Man that I have a gun I'll know just who to deal with.'

The next morning at about 8.30 the third mate came with a notice which he pinned in the foc'sle for all to read. The notice read:

Extract from the Official Log Book[*]

E. Marke, J. James and D. Forest, all firemen, came to me and complained about their food. Marke, who was the spokesman, used abusive language to me and told me I should have had fresh meat, which at sea the law doesn't call for as the ship is not equipped for that purpose. The men refused to raise steam beyond 150 lbs. The steam pressure being 190 lbs., the coal being good and the ship on time charter, I regard this shortage of steam as serious. I intend to prosecute these men to the full extent of the law on arrival at Panama or a United States port.

Signed E. W. Raper

---

[*] This is, in fact, an exact copy of the original.

Looking at the faces of the sea-lawyers I could see they were very frightened. I knew I had to do some dramatic acting. I beckoned to John James, one of my watchmates who was still having his breakfast, to follow me on to the deck. With a serious face I left the foc'sle and made my way out. A moment later John joined me.

'Look here,' I whispered, 'I want you to go back in the foc'sle, looking as serious as you can and say, Marke has gone barmy and has taken this very seriously! He just told me that he really intends to kill the first three men who will dare to raise the steam any higher.'

He went back.

I sat on the top of a hatch, my chin resting pensively on my fist. I knew that soon the four to eight stokers would be on deck on their way to the bathroom, facing the hatch. As they passed by I raised my eyes and looked squarely at the two sea-lawyers. And from what I saw in their eyes as they met mine, I knew that everything would go according to plan.

After three or four days of this, the Old Man sent for me. He asked me what was the grievance for this shortage of steam. I told him that the first cause was the food, but our real grievance began when the chief mate thought he could settle everything by sheer bullying and threat, that's all there was to it.

The captain said he was very surprised at our conduct and added, 'You men have been with me over a year; have I ever been mean or bad to any of you?'

'No, sir,' I answered truthfully.

Then he explained the reason for the absence of fresh meat, and went on courteously, 'Listen, Marke, this ship is on time charter and unless we get to New York in time we lose the charter. Already four days have been wasted. The coal is good, if you go to work now and shake her up we can still make it and I shall forget this ever happened. What do you say?'

'If you think we can still make it, then we'll make it, sir,' I said with sincerity, 'You can rely on me.' I smiled feebly, turned round smartly and left. There were no witnesses to this scene. Our conversation took place in the captain's cabin.

I have never been unaware of the fact that there are many people who would work or do the right thing only by being forced or bullied into doing it. But these are definitely the minority. It's my conviction that a firm but understanding boss could get the best out of anybody without threat. The Old Man had spoken to me like a human being with common-sense and I appreciated it.

I went back to the foc'sle and told the men exactly what the captain said. I asked them to shake her up and give her everything she was worth. Then I went down to the stokehold and told the men on watch the same. The coal was good as the captain had said, the weather was good as usual in the Pacific, and we were all first-class stokers who were not afraid of work. Within half an hour of my leaving the captain's cabin the ship had gathered her usual speed of twelve knots, and some more. And now she was gracefully ploughing the ocean with her full capacity.

We arrived in New York twenty-four hours before time. The captain kept his word as we knew he would. And the chief officer never interfered with us any more.

6

MY LIFE AS A CROCUSER

When I finally left the *Manchester Civilian*, I decided to quit the sea for good and go into business on my own account. With the help of my wife and a troupe of six including myself, I started a side show at Coney Beach, Porthcawl, on half shares with Mr Johnny Crole, the well-known West of England entertainment boss. But at the end of the season I was at a loss through lack of experience. I was paying out too high a wage to the troupe and letting the performance run too long. I was so discouraged by this that I decided to leave show business and go out working in the markets crocusing (quack doctoring). That way I wouldn't have any wages to pay, except fares and market tolls.

A well-known northern crocuser gave me a prescription of certain medicinal herbs and pills. He also introduced me to one of the leading wholesale chemists in Britain where I could have my regular supply cheap. I had labels with my name and address printed on every package and directions how to use.

I was now on my own, but I was soon to find out that selling medicine wasn't as easy as I'd thought; in fact, I found out that it was about the hardest thing to sell in market places.

Unless one knew what one was talking about and believed in oneself, or at least knew how to convince the audience of one's sincerity, one couldn't sell five shillings' worth a week.

And what's more, you might be a real doctor of medicine with all the diplomas in the world, and yet it wouldn't help you to sell a single packet if you didn't know how to 'bat'; that is to say, you must know the psychological moment to stop the spiel and start the selling. You could lose a whole day's takings by being one moment too early or one moment too late.

After weeks of hard work with no return, I was just about to pack it up when I came across a coloured man whom I'd always admired for his work and his very smart appearance. This was the late 'Professor' Edgar B. Knight, the great Abyssinian herbalist who died at Wombwell, Yorkshire, in the early thirties. He told me if I wished to sell medicine I was certainly going the wrong way about it. He asked for the recipe and I told him; he said it was very good, in fact the best for the particular ailments, but that wasn't the important part, not if I wanted to sell them.

He told me all about the credulity of the public. 'But,' he said, 'gullible as they are, they wouldn't buy a genuine brick of gold for five shillings if you're only going to tell them the plain truth that it is gold and it's genuine. You've to tell them more than that and prove it!'

I asked, 'How could anyone prove, on the spot, that a particular medicine is good? Surely no one takes medicine and gets well on the spot, no matter how good.'

He replied, 'That's what you think. I shall be at Sheffield Market tomorrow morning, be there with your swag (stock) and I'll show you what I mean.'

He shook hands with me. 'I must be leaving you now,' he said placidly, 'I have to call on a patient.'

I had known Knight even before I left the sea. He was a friend of my wife's family and I'd heard of his ability as a man of medicine but I'd never actually seen him at work.

I met him the next morning at Sheffield as arranged. He was immaculately dressed, as ever, striped trousers, black jacket and so on, just as one would expect of a doctor. We walked towards his stall.

'Place four dozen packets of your herbs on the stall,' he said. 'And watch me get rid of them for you in one pitch.'*

---

* A collection of people.

He pulled out a paper bag; in it was five pounds' worth of silver which he emptied on the stall.

'Do you know why I placed all that money on the stall?' he asked, his eyes level with mine.

'For change,' I said innocently.

'Yes, it could be,' he remarked, 'but that isn't the main reason.' He winked roguishly. 'It's to indicate that my medicine is good; if it wasn't I wouldn't have been able to sell all that much even before I began to spiel.'

'B . . But . . .' I stuttered.

'Yes, I know what you're about to say,' he interrupted, 'I haven't sold anything yet; you know it and I know it. But does the public know it?' He then asked me to stand about four feet away in front of the stall and watch him. This I did.

While muttering to himself and removing packets of herbs and pills from one end of the stall to the other end and bringing back the same packets from where he'd taken them, all of which seemed silly to me, I noticed that a crowd was already gathering, and within ten minutes there were about twenty people behind me, all watching with interest and wondering what he was doing. All this time his back was towards us.

Slowly he turned round and began to spiel. Within another ten minutes there were about seventy-five people around his stall. And by the end of the next fifteen minutes he had sold more than six pounds' worth of pills. He then dispersed the crowd by thanking them in his suave and perfect English. This they respected, voicing their thoughts that he was indeed an educated man.

A few minutes later another crowd had gathered. This time he switched on to a different form of patter, something about how to attack a certain poison which sometimes accumulates in one's blood. So that they could see with their own eyes how this poison accumulates he performed an experiment with a glass of water to which he added a drop of yellow liquid from a green bottle marked 'poison', which he said was the poison which causes certain illness. The clear water then instantly turned to inky blackness.

Pointing his gold fountain pen at the audience he looked them straight in the eye. 'Because nearly everything you eat in our modern society contains chemical I doubt if there is anyone standing here now who hasn't got a trace of this poison in his blood. There's only one way you can get rid of the poison, and I now intend to show you. Please watch me carefully.'

From an open packet of herbs he took half a teaspoonful and emptied it into the black substance in the glass. Soon the water was clear, apart from the sediment. He kept his eyes on the glass all the time while the water was being 'purified', saying at the same time, ' Watch how the antidote works; yes, it works wonders my friends! As it destroys the poison in this glass so would it destroy the poison in your system.' He went on, 'This particular herb only grows in my country and this is the first time it is being introduced to the Western world. Only one man in England could supply you with it.'

He shook his head regretfully. ' Oh no, not I; even I couldn't do that, at least not yet.'

He pointed to me. ' This is the man! He's a cousin of mine just arrived in this country a few weeks ago with a limited supply of the herbs. If he wanted to make money out of you he would gladly charge you one pound a packet and you would gladly buy it because it's good. But the herbs cost him practically nothing apart from customs' duty, packages and travelling expenses. He has a free supply of it from our grandfather who happens to be the chief medicine man of our tribe. He asks me to charge you just one shilling a packet and two and sixpence for three packets. He couldn't supply every one of you, for that is absolutely out of the question! But I think he has enough here to supply half of you. You will find the directions on the packet. I will start from my left and walk towards my right. Thank you.'

Ten minutes later all the four dozen packets I had laid out were gone.

After the performance I said to him, ' I know that my herbs are good, the chemist said so and you said so; but I never thought it could clear poison away so quickly.'

He looked at me, smiled and said coldly, ' That my boy, is the trick of the trade.'

Professor E. B. Knight, the great Abyssinian herbalist, was in fact not an Abyssinian at all. He was born in Demerara, Guyana (the former British Guiana), and had never been in any part of Africa; yet when he wasn't immaculately dressed in Western clothes he was dressed in expensive African robes; that was part of his gimmick.

He told me he never would have been half as successful if the public had known that he was from the Western world. Since he was a herbalist, he said, and herbs being nature's medicine, he had to present himself as a son of nature; for only then would they look up to him and believe in him.

' And I'll tell you something else; everyone who takes my medicine will be sure to find improvement in his health. It matters not if my medicine is good, they'll find it good because I have impressed them and made them believe.'

This was no idle boast. In one particular case that I can still clearly remember, a woman of distinction once stopped and listened to Knight lecturing to a crowd of people at Barnsley market, Yorkshire. She was so impressed that she wouldn't leave till she'd had a private conversation with him. This lady, who was suffering from a certain complaint, told Knight all about it. According to her she'd consulted all the best doctors there were, including a specialist, all to no avail. And now she was ready to place herself in Knight's care, for as she said, ' I've nothing to lose.'

Within three months the lady admitted she'd never felt better in her life and couldn't thank him enough.

In Wombwell where he had a marvellous practice he was well liked by everybody including all the children, who used to follow him about. He was the only negro living in the town as far as I can remember.

There were only three negroes at his funeral, Big Morris, my sister-in-law and myself, but he had the grandest funeral I'd ever seen at any small town. All the flags in the town were at half mast, all the schools had the day off in order to attend the funeral, and the pall-bearers were members of the British Legion. He had served in the First World War with distinction. Days after his death the Yorkshire newspapers were still full of articles about him. He would have been very proud to see his own funeral for he was a proud and generous man. May he rest in peace.

After that morning with Knight at Sheffield market, back home in Manchester, with the aid of a dictionary and a few medical terms which I borrowed from Knight, I wrote down a ' fanny ' (speech). I read it over and over again till I could say it backwards with my eyes closed, but not word for word. I walked up and down my bedroom for days talking to myself till my wife began to get suspicious of my losing my sanity and wanted to call in a doctor.

But when I finally went back on the markets I began to take money. Within a few months I had so much confidence I imagined myself to be a real doctor, and what's more my audience began to look up to me.

Whenever I was out working, after every pitch people would sidle up to me and tell me their inner secrets; orders began coming through the post, even people who had never seen me began writing for my herbs and advice, mentioning that my address was passed on to them. I began to like my work. I met other crocusers and exchanged views.

I made lots of money on this racket but I never kept it. Market grafters, like gamblers, seldom do; yet I don't think there are any nicer or more easy-going people. They're always ready to give advice or a helping hand to a newcomer. But talk about the angler and the one that got away, you couldn't beat the market grafter for boasting! He's for ever telling the other bloke about a wonderful gaff he went to the other day: ' I had an execution! (big crowd) And when I handed out I had about four hundred punters in that one pitch, the next pitch was even better.'

Funny thing, some of these grafters sell very good medicine though they may not even know it themselves.

The following are true incidents in every detail, told by Leo Rudolph, the well-known market journalist who used to write for the *World's Fair* (Grafters' Corner). Leo himself was born in the business.

A well-known crocuser had been suffering from a certain ailment for ages. Though he sold a cure for this particular ailment he wouldn't take it himself. Instead, he tried every remedy under the sun, visited all kinds of real doctors, but all to no avail. In desperation he decided to try his own medicine. No one was more surprised than he when he was cured.

Another crocuser suffered for ages in silence, but rather than take his own medicine he went to see a real doctor who gave him a box of pills and told him it was the latest on the market. The pills cured him. But he went raving mad when he later discovered it was the same brand of pills he had been selling for donkey's years. He figured he'd been 'gazoomped'.* Those were the days when you had to pay the doctor's fee.

It wasn't long after I started on the medicine lark that I met Black Dougie. Dougie came from Jamaica, but he worked as an African. He was well educated, a master of words in the English language, and very dark with a pugnacious look. And having a wonderful set of teeth he made more money with his home-made tooth powder than with anything else.

'In Africa where I come from,' he'd spiel, 'we clean our teeth with this very preparation! The root powder in it protects both gums and teeth, with the result that false teeth are absolutely unknown amongst my people. In fact, if I could take my teeth from my mouth and replace them in the presence of my people I would be acclaimed and accepted immediately as the greatest witch-doctor in all Africa! Furthermore, with the teeth in my hand where I could see them face to face, like some of you could do, you can rest assured that after one use of this preparation they would glitter so much even the stars above would envy me!'

He had a dry sense of humour which often kept his audience roaring with laughter. Once at Doncaster market he had a large crowd around him and was selling his herbs, chest mixture and tooth powder like hot cakes, with a running commentary. At the next stall was a big northern crocuser who thought Dougie was taking away all his customers. He lost his temper and shouted out at Dougie: 'Bah gum, Sambo, if thou don't shut mouth Ah'll coom and shut it for thee.'

Dougie slowly looked round, gave the man a cold, aggressive stare and retorted calmly, 'Bah gum, thou art a bleeding liar!' And while the audience were laughing their heads off he turned slowly round again, resumed his running commentary and made a clean sell-out.

Dougie and I had always been friends. When we met at a gaff where there was only room for one of us to work, we just

---

* robbed.

teamed up and shared the takings regardless of whose swag was used.

Dougie, for all his aggressive looks, was easy-going and very generous. He wouldn't see any market grafter in trouble. In fact he had more friends on the markets than any man I knew.

A gang of hooligans once set on him and beat him up at a northern market. Within hours he'd found out who they were and where they usually hung around. The next day Dougie marched into the town leading an army of white men, sought out the gang and nearly pulverized the lot of them. The news went round and no mob ever took a liberty with Dougie after that.

A few years ago, just before he died, even though he was all grey on the head and suffering from ill-health which he tried to hide, I noticed that he was still independent and wouldn't tolerate anyone who crashed his company without formal introduction.

It was during one of my visits to Manchester where he lived. We decided to go to a nearby public house for a quiet drink and talk about old times. We hadn't quite sat down at a corner table when a seedy-looking character came in. His eyes went all round the premises and rested on us. Immediately he started pushing his way towards us as if we were his two long-lost brothers. It was so obvious we couldn't help noticing it. At first I thought he was a friend of Dougie's.

He pulled a chair to our table and sat down. And without even a good evening he started talking vigorously. ' You know, there's a lotta people in this country who don't like you people, they think you're not equal to us. You know wut I call it? Prejudice! Colour prejudice – that's wut.'

He pushed his face towards me as far as it would go. ' But I say that you're as good as me, an' I'll always say so. Black or no black you're as good as the next man – bah gum!'

My eyes must have been round in astonishment as I looked at him.

He stretched out a generous hand to Dougie. ' Shake 'ands, Sambo. I'm not too proud to shake 'ands with thee – why should I be – you're as good as me, ain't you?' Answering his own question he jerked his head and winked, ' Oh – ah.'

While I was flabbergasted and couldn't find words, Dougie

gave him the coldest, blackest look I'd ever seen and said icily, 'My dear good fellow, you barged in here, pushing everybody out of your way to get to this table when there are other tables vacant; then you picked up a chair and made yourself comfortable without any introduction whatever! And like the head of the Ministry of Propaganda you started, with thunderous verbosity, to infuse into our incompetent brains the most valuable of all information that we are as good as you! That's nice of you.' Suddenly he pushed his face towards the man, eyeball to eyeball nearly touching his face. He barked, 'Very well! But now tell me, what the goddamn blazing hell made you think that you are as good as us?'

This sudden movement and barking nearly cause the man to fall off his seat. He couldn't leave quickly enough.

That's just like Dougie, he was always ready for the occasion.

There used to be quite a number of coloured men with colourful characters, grafting the markets and race courses. But now they are all dead, including my old pal the great Prince Monululu, and as for me, I have retired now.

There was 'Dr' Lascelles from Sierra Leone, tall, black as ebony, with a commanding appearance. When Lascelles walked in the streets, everybody looked. We were shipmates once, but he left the sea before I did and started grafting lucky charms, dressed in spectacular Eastern costume; he called his charm 'Ragai' which he said was the Goddess of Fortune. He did very well at this, but his goal was medicine.

He saved and bought all kinds of books on osteology and studied very hard. Then he went to Ireland where he wasn't known and opened a practice as an osteopath and masseur, with a secretary and two nurses for a flash. He did very well. But after some years he was charged with performing an illegal operation and causing the death of the patient, which he strongly denied. He was sentenced to eighteen months; he appealed and the sentence was doubled.

He lost everything he'd built up, but he wasn't the type of man to give up easily. He came back to England and teamed up with me for a while flipping* on the races. While I spent my share, he saved his and went back to Ireland where the

---

* tipping.

people still loved him. He was soon back in business, but he was a sick man after that prison sentence. He carried on only through sheer guts and determination.

There was Big Morris from Jamaica. He too was once a shipmate of mine, who quit the sea at the same time. A gentler man one never saw, but he wasn't much of a grafter because he wasn't original and was always imitating some other grafter. He dressed exactly like Monululu. In fact he copied every item of Monululu's costume, even the horse shoe around his neck and the 'I got an 'orse' cry. And being the same build as Monululu and the same shade of colour, people would flock around him thinking he was Monululu. And he never told them he wasn't. For this Monululu hated him like poison.

I often watched Monululu's face when Morris was around; if black looks could kill, Morris would have been dead long before.

Now we come to another character: Peter Jackson from Nigeria. He worked under the name of Prince Zalemka. And neither was he one of Monululu's close buddies. He dressed like Monululu but that was as far as it went. He hadn't the slightest resemblance to Monululu. In fact he was short and stocky, with a much darker complexion. No one in his right senses would have mistaken him for Monululu. Nor did he want them to.

With mouth wide open like a yawning hippopotamus, eyes rolling like a Kentucky minstrel, Peter would proclaim loudly, 'I am not Monululu.' Thumbing his chest, he'd vociferate, 'I am Prince Zalemka! A better man!'

He was always generous with his big broad smile, but that was all anybody could get out of him. Peter was so mean that if he'd had a park he wouldn't have allowed a bird to sing in it – if the bird wasn't a blonde. That was his weakness, blondes! Blondes, blondes, any blonde so long as she was game; the smile would get broader and the pound notes would be coming up like he had manufactured them. I'll give him his due, he wouldn't ask a penny from anybody. He always had a big roll hidden on his person anyway. He certainly was a character.

On the St Leger day, 1932, something unpleasant happened. I was grafting the races at Doncaster and was doing very well.

I had already tipped two good winners and the last pitch had just dispersed. I was preparing to start another when three tough-looking fellows swaggered up to me.

Said one of them, 'Oi, darky, we just backed a loser and we're stony broke and wanna go 'ome. Gie us a nicker for our fare will you? That's all we want.'

Now I'm the softest person in the world for a touch; anyone with a hard luck story can get anything out of me. Many a time after saying what a fool I'd been, within twenty-four hours I'd be dipping my hands in my pockets and doing the same thing over again. But threats or blackmail I could never tolerate. I'd given many a down-and-out stranger a 'tosh' or a 'caiser' (2s 6d or 5s) without even thinking of it. But I didn't like the attitude of these men; furthermore they were asking for a pound just like that; a pound was a lot in those days.

As I was about to ask what they meant, up came a fourth man who looked an even bigger villain than the others.

He leered at me and said to another one of them, 'Wasser marrer, 'Arry, don't 'e wanna fork out?'

By this time I was crowded by the four of them.

'Look 'ere, Sambo,' said one, 'we don't wanna get tough wi' you, do we now? Didn't you 'ear us tell the people on your last pitch that you jus' gave us a blooming big winner? Bloody 'ell, wha' you think we did that for, our 'ealth?'

I told them to go to hell. And soon I found myself on the ground and being kicked from all angles. However, there were screams from the women around, who started hitting them with their shoes. This frightened them away. I was only slightly bruised and soon dismissed the incident. However, while having a drink that same night in a pub at the market square, I went to use the toilet which was situated in the yard, when four men followed and attacked me. I fought back vigorously and desperately. Fortunately for me a man coming out to use the toilet saw this. He rushed back into the pub and raised the alarm. The women then started shouting and pushing their menfolk out into the yard to help me. This frightened my assailants and they ran off. But by this time I had received two fractured ribs, a broken nose and a few cuts on the face. Still they didn't get any money out of me if that was what they were after. But it was quite some time after that before I was fit to go to work.

On returning to Doncaster the following year I was informed by the locals at the market square that the leader of that mob was an ex-police officer who had been fired from the Doncaster police force a few years before. How true that was I had no way of knowing, but I have often wondered if they were the same mob who had attacked me earlier that day at the races. I didn't have time to look at their faces and it was dark. But it wouldn't have mattered anyway because I wouldn't have reported it. If I had to inform the police every time I was attacked by hooligans they would be so busy hunting them down that they would be snoring while working, for lack of sleep.

But for years after that I carried a loaded revolver in my pocket when working the races; some people who have never been in my position and don't have my colour, would call this irresponsible. That's a matter of opinion. However, fortunately for me and them, no race-course mob has attacked me since then.

I came down to London on Derby Sunday, 1933. I went straight to Epsom Downs and started grafting. I was tipping Hyperion to win the Derby because I'd seen it run and win earlier on at Chester. On that form I didn't think there was anything to beat it on the Derby, and my calculation was right. Hyperion won.

I made a lot of money tipping on the Sunday, Tuesday and on the Derby day before the big race, simply because many knew that I'd tipped April the Fifth the year before to win the Derby and it did. Apart from a few shillings which I laid out on other horses, I saved everything for the Derby; so when Hyperion passed the post I was a good winner.

That night I decided to visit the famous Soho I'd heard so much talk about. After having a few drinks around the boozers I felt good and asked someone to take me to a club. I was taken to a gambling club somewhere in Dean Street. I wasn't looking for that kind of club but seeing a poker game in session, a game I'd always loved, I decided to take a hand. That was one of the silliest mistakes I'd ever made and I've made plenty. They were all Greek-Cypriots playing amongst themselves and there was I a total stranger playing with them; and there's very little anyone can teach a Greek gambler.

' I was a stranger and they took me in,' is the best expression to describe what happened. By 6 am, with the exception of the roll of money, which I'd put aside in a separate pocket for the wife, I was stone broke. By this time I'd sobered up and discovered that the cards were marked, every one of them. All the packs had been marked before they were opened in front of me at the table.

I didn't squeal. That would have done me no good except make more trouble as I had a loaded gun in my pocket which I might have been forced to use. I took the wife's money and starting playing cool and memorizing every mark on the cards. I was now playing to an advantage. By 10 am I'd won back about a quarter of my money but then they suddenly called off the game. I think they'd got wise to me.

I tried to lure them by telling them that what I'd lost was nothing to what I still had in my pocket, but they wouldn't fall for the bait. I didn't have to understand Greek to know what they were talking about. Anyway, that's how I came to live in London and took to professional gambling in Soho. I might add that I not only won back my money in the years to come but I made a lot of profit. I even became partner in a couple of gambling clubs later with two of the Cypriots who had cheated me.

I got on very well with them and there were never any hard feelings. In any case I'd only myself to blame, and besides they did me a favour, for if it wasn't for my trying to get even with them I wouldn't have been living in London today. Now I love London so much I would hate to leave it. I've had many ups and downs in this city but it has accelerated my education.

New York, Philadelphia, Chicago, are all fast cities; but the wide boys in these cities, apart from their guns, could still learn a thing or two from the wide boys in London.

Because I was like a rolling stone I couldn't stick to one thing too long. Sometimes when I got fed up with shuffling cards all night and breathing foul air, I'd take to the open markets and race courses, get some air into my lungs, then after a spell of bad weather I'd find myself back in the gambling dens.

While I was on one of my market spells Old Man Trouble struck again. After finishing a hard day's graft at an East End market, crocusing, I realized that my stock needed replenishing. I couldn't afford to replenish it with the money I had in hand as there were other obligations to settle, so I decided to go to Soho and do a spot of gambling. Up to then all my gambling activities in London had been with white people. Mostly Greeks, Maltese and Jews, but this evening I found myself in a basement club among my own people, in Carlisle Street, Soho Square.

A little stud poker was in progress. I joined in. Though they were all coloured boys playing, I was a stranger amongst them. I played for over four hours without winning a hand, then the luck changed: I played for an inside straight and made it. The odds on making this kind of hand are slim and poker players seldom go in for it. But I was losing and desperate, took a chance and made it. That was all there was to it; but I won the pot from a man who had been losing the whole night and wasn't in a good mood.

He gave me a mean look. 'Something bloody fishy going on round here,' he growled. 'If anything like it happens again, someone will get a bloody punch right in the bleeding nose!'

I said nothing even though I knew he was referring to me. I had a two-year-old daughter, Sheila, who was with her mother in Manchester, and trouble was the last thing in the world I wanted. But when trouble was one's shadow one just couldn't dodge it. That's just how I was to see the inside of my first London prison.

A few deals later I beat him again when he had a good hand. This was too much for him. He accused me of cheating. And I called him a bad loser and warned him to watch his tongue. Then he jumped from his seat and threw a punch at me but it didn't really hurt me for I saw it coming and rode it. He followed up by hitting me with a chair. In trying to avoid the force of the blow one of my fingers got fractured. He was in a rage. And my temper had also begun to rise. And since there wasn't a friendly face in sight I thought it was time he and his associates knew I had a gun.

As he made the second attack I warned him to drop the chair or I would have to shoot him. But not seeing a gun in my hand he ignored the warning and rushed me. Quickly I flashed out the gun and fired a warning shot between his legs.

He wasn't hit but the explosion and sight of the gun checked him. Now that I had made my point I became cool and collected. Then one of the men shouted, 'Don't let him bluff you, Paul. It's a dummy with blanks.' Paul renewed the attack.

This time I aimed at one of his legs and fired. The bullet missed but it went through his trouser leg and grazed him. By the look on Paul's face everyone knew then that it was a real gun with live bullets, and now there was great confusion as they scrambled for the door – each for himself and God for all. Now that I was in command of the situation I was even more calm; I always was when I pulled a gun at anybody. I would never want to kill, at least not if I could help it. But I also knew that whatever happened now I was in trouble with the law – a trouble forced on me. So I might as well go to jail for something.

I took a position with my back to the wall, took aim at one of Paul's legs and fired. But because he was nearest to the concrete wall at the side of the door, this bullet hit the concrete and bounced back and hit one of the men on the mouth, scattering some of his teeth. As he fell on the floor, bleeding profusely, I thought that was the end of him. But he lived to tell the tale later.

Not knowing at this time that it was a ricochet bullet that had hit the man, I was surprised and shocked. Soon everyone had disappeared, leaving the shot man behind lying in a pool of blood. And now I was seized with fear, thinking I'd killed him.

I rushed out into the street and headed towards Oxford Street, and soon I was home after taking three different taxis in a roundabout way. But less than three hours later the house was surrounded by the flying squad. How they discovered where I lived and so quickly was a big surprise to me – even though I was thinking of surrendering myself and facing the consequences. The one thing in the world I could never bear was to be a wanted man. I would rather be hanged and finished with than have to dodge the police the rest of my life.

Soon I was taken to Vine Street police station where I was questioned and charged with the attempted murder of Benjamin Byer and Paul Burnett. It was hard for Inspector Edwards, who was in charge of the case, to believe I was shooting low – especially since there was a witness who claimed I was threatening to kill everybody. And since I could not explain how a bullet came to hit Benjamin Byer on the face, it looked like I was going to prison for a long time. Still it was a relief to know the man wasn't killed.

But the inspector was the fairest policeman I'd ever met. Long before the trial, he made a thorough examination of the club premises, including measurements, and found that my story of the shooting was true in every detail.

After a preliminary hearing by the late Mr Sandbach at Marlborough Street police court, I was sent to the Old Bailey. The police gave a very fair and unprejudiced statement at the trial and I was sent in for only nine months. But because gun fights in England in those days were few and far between, the betting amongst the Soho gamblers was that I'd get a sentence of four to seven years.

After serving three days in gaol, the governor sent for me. When he began to tell me the court had decided to alter my sentence I nearly dropped dead waiting for him to finish what he had to say, for only that morning one of the prisoners had told me during exercise that the judge must have made a mistake writing down nine months when he meant nine years. When the governor went on to tell me that three months had been deducted, which meant I would now have to do six months instead of the nine, I was stupefied. A moment later I recovered my senses, grinned broadly and gave him a smart salute. ' Oh, thank you sir!'

I had one month's remission and came out after doing five months.

In fairness to the men with whom I tangled, I must add that they never bore any grudge whatever against me. Until Benjamin Byer died, which was only quite recently, we gossiped and drank whenever we met. Paul Burnett is now back in his own country in Eastern Nigeria, running a hotel and club in

Calabar. And whenever he is in England on business he always calls to see me and we have a drink and chat about old times. He is a very young sixty-five. The last time we met was as recently as 1973.

The biggest scare I'd ever had in my life was when I did something definitely against my principles: carrying a loaded gun on my person, knowing full well I was going out to get drunk. Even though I'd carried a loaded gun on and off for quite a number of years I never did so if there was a possibility of my getting drunk. I had seen too many men shot down by drunken men when I was in the States. I had also seen many drunks get shot down for talking out of turn or starting a row with the wrong person. I'd realized that a loaded gun was indeed a dangerous thing which should never at any cost be carried by a hasty person, a drunk or a coward. I'd subdued bad men and bullies with the point of a loaded gun at least a dozen times. But on every occasion I'd been cool, collected and sober.

It was during the early part of the last war. I was a croupier at a gambling club in Brewer Street, Soho, owned by the late Harry Etting, who later bought a wholly legitimate business in the Edgware Road district after the war and became very successful.

Business was very bad that night; there were just a few people in the club, some having something to eat, some drinking soft drinks, and no one seemed to want to get on the gaming tables, which, after all, were the business. About 1 am a bevy of girls I knew came down and had something to eat. As they were leaving I was invited to go along with them to a birthday party which one of them was having in her flat. At first I refused. But after a little persuasion, and sensing there would be no business that night anyway, I decided to string along. We all crammed into a taxi and drove towards Paddington.

There were lots of drinks in the flat but I only wanted rum. A full bottle of rum was then offered me and I was told to finish the lot if I could as no one else in the party was a rum drinker. The last thing I remembered was draining the last drop in the bottle.

When I became conscious I found myself in a cell. After realizing where I was, my first impulse was to feel for my gun which of course had already been taken by the police. I tried to think of what had happened but all I could remember was that I'd been at a party somewhere in Paddington and I'd been draining the last drop from a bottle of Lemon Hart rum. Try as I might, I just couldn't remember anything else.

When the door of the cell was opened so that I could be taken from Paddington police station, where I was incarcerated, to Marylebone magistrates' court, I asked what the charge was and was told that I'd find out soon enough.

All the way to Marylebone I was in torture. By the time I arrived at Marylebone and was ushered into another cell I couldn't stand it any longer. I banged on the cell door for all I was worth. A police officer asked what I wanted.

'What is the nature of my charge apart from being drunk?' I asked apprehensively.

He replied quite solemnly, 'You're asking me; don't you know? Well, if you don't, you'll know soon enough.'

This shocked my headache away, and in its place was a terrible feeling. I felt like it was the end of the road. Have I killed somebody? That was the question I was asking myself and the answer kept coming to my sick brain: I must have done.

I banged on the door again. At the appearance of an officer, I asked the same question. 'What am I here for . . . ?'

And I had the same answer: 'You'll know soon enough.'

By then I was going mad and if I hadn't tried to control myself I would have banged on that door till I was carried out.

After about three hours, which seemed to me like three years, the cell door opened and I was ushered before the magistrate. When the charge was read and the question asked how did I plead, I couldn't answer for a moment for the shock; only it wasn't fear but ease and satisfaction – instead of hearing what I'd dreaded, the charge was of being drunk and disorderly and possessing a firearm and ammunition without a permit. When the question was repeated I found my voice and quickly pleaded guilty. I was given a three months' sentence, which I served with pleasure. I learned later how I came to be arrested. Having finished the bottle of rum I felt hot, took off my jacket and started dancing by myself. Seeing the butt of my gun, which was now exposed from my hip pocket, the guests (all of whom were white) became restless. Some began to leave the premises, others manoeuvred to keep away from me. Thinking I was being snubbed because of my colour I became aggressive and insulted some of them. Then I picked up my jacket and stormed out. I was arrested soon after.

After this dreadful experience I made a solemn promise to myself that I'd never own another gun. But there is a universal saying which is common amongst my people back home: 'Man proposes. God disposes.' And so it happened that on my way to work one evening soon after my release, I felt awfully thirsty and dropped into a pub at Great Windmill Street for a quick one.

No sooner had I walked to the bar when some white GIs took offence to my presence. (American troops had just begun to arrive in England.)

'See wha' we got here; a goddamn nigger!' said one of them. And they closed in on me.

'Listen here nigger,' one said with a cynical grin. 'If you know wha's good for you you'll leave this place an' run.' The others were glaring at me with hatred in their eyes.

Before I had time to answer I was dragged from the bar and thrown into the street.

'We don't drink in the same place with niggers, not where we come from.'

I went sprawling on the pavement and nearly fractured my skull. Blood started streaming down my face. For a moment I felt like going back and letting them finish the job, but then I thought more wisely of it and walked away, humiliated. I had just been called up for the army. Now I decided they would have to come and get me. 'Let them fight the bloody war themselves,' I told myself angrily. 'It's a white man's war and I'm having none of it.' I was so infuriated I made up my mind there and then to buy another gun. For the next four or five hours I was in nearly every shady club in Soho looking for one. I was willing to pay any amount for any gun as long as it could shoot to kill, but I wasn't lucky that night – or was I? I just couldn't get one, not even on loan, but within forty-eight hours I'd found and bought one. By this time, however, I'd cooled down.

Instead of going back to the pub to shoot any American who happened to be there as I'd intended, I tried to forget the whole incident thought it wasn't easy. In fact from that evening until the end of the war, after most of the GIs had been sent back home, I kept away from all pubs.

7

SOHO DAYS

Since I seldom keep records, apart from important documents and my seaman's discharge book in which the character of the holder is registered, I cannot be sure of the time of this amusing and ironic episode, except that it was during the last war when loads of American troops were arriving in Britain. I had wanted to open a club in Soho and while looking round for suitable premises I spread the news around as advance publicity. That was how my association with Smart Alec began.

I had just entered a restaurant at Bateman Street with three friends one afternoon when a tall, impressive-looking African I knew walked in. He came towards my table and asked if he could talk to me outside for a moment. 'It's urgent business that can't wait; I've been looking for you all over the place.'

Walking out of the restaurant he added, 'I hear you're looking for premises to open a club.'

'That's right,' I replied, 'Do you know of any vacant premises in a good position?'

He did not reply. Instead he asked, 'What kind of a club do you want to open?'

'A gaming club of course, what else?'

Then he began, 'I don't want to interfere in your business, but listen, man, what kind of money can you make in gambling right now? It's a risky business and, besides, who would you get in your club except a gang of cheap ponces who are liable to raise a lot of Cain when they lose a couple of pounds. Then what happens? you end up in gaol. Now I've got a proposition, a sound proposition, but I don't want to talk too much. I'm a man that believes in action. Can you spare half an hour, maybe less? I just want to take you to some place round the corner and show you something. Tell your friends to wait. We'll be right back.'

I went back to the restaurant and gave the waiter enough money to cover whatever my friends might have, and told him he could keep the change. I then went back to the table and asked my friends to excuse me for a while and not to leave before my return.

On our way to St Martin's Lane, where my acquaintance was taking me, he started telling me in his impressive way:

'Listen, Marke, a war is on and the Yanks are here, but the war can't last for ever. There's only one way for you to make quick money right now and I can tell you it's not by gambling, it's by drinking. Who wants to gamble at present? Not the Yanks; they want to drink and have a good time before they get killed and they are the men with the dough who will spend and like it, not these damn cheap ponces round here.'

He went on, 'Now there's a fellow who wants to sell his drinking club but we don't want it; it's a little one-room affair in St Martin's Lane where we're going now; it couldn't even hold ten people. He couldn't sell it for dirt; but what we want is his licence, which he wouldn't part with for less than seventy-five pounds even though it only cost him five shillings. If I had any money I wouldn't be looking for you. Now if you buy that licence I'll find you the premises, you can bet on that. All I want in return is a promise of a permanent job when you open. I want to be the receptionist and your right-hand man. And believe me, I'll show you how to make quick money.'

It was indeed a little, one-room affair. There was nobody on the premises except the proprietor, a little man from Portugal whom I shall call Mr de Goldini. The chairs and tables were all piled up in one corner with cobwebs all over them, proving it must have been a long time since anybody had had a drink there.

'Mr de Goldini, I want you to meet Mr Marke, my partner,'

said my guide, and I didn't contradict the partnership business. I just shook hands with the man and he started talking.

'Before de war alla my customer Italian. Now alla gone Internment camp. So I no open no more. No customer.'

He forged on, 'I tink de gentle-amana a tella you I gotta licen, yes? You giva me seventy-five pounds, I giva you de licen.'

He produced the licence and showed it to me. It was up to date.

'But,' he went on, 'Me I no parta wid de licen, I parta only when you giva me de seventy-five pounds. I no supposa sell, you no supposa buy; so I parta only, when you giva me de seventy-five pounds.'

My new partner interrupted, 'Aye, take it easy, Mr de Goldini, you talk like you're dealing with two shady characters. We are gentlemen, that's what we are, gentlemen.'

Mr de Goldini countered, 'Oh yes, sir, in Soho everybody gentleman. But I talka jus's same.'

On leaving the premises I told the man not to worry; we wouldn't want his licence before he received his seventy-five pounds. I told him that he probably would not see me again but my 'partner' would see him when we were ready for it.

As we went out, I agreed with my friend that his proposition was sound and that I would fall in with it. But I had no intention of paying even a shilling for a piece of paper which would be quite worthless if we didn't have the right premises. Until then he must keep in with the man and see that he didn't sell it anywhere else. With regard to his premises, I wouldn't take over his place if I were paid, to which sentiment he agreed.

'You leave that to me, he can't sell that licence until we are ready for it.'

With that I gave him my phone number, left him and joined my party.

Here was the type of man who wouldn't let grass grow under his feet. The very next morning I was preparing for bed when the phone rang. It was my partner asking me to meet him. He had good news. I got dressed again and went out to meet him. He showed me a large empty building in New Compton Street which he said was to let, although there was no placard to that effect. He even gave me the name of the landlord, his address and phone number.

The landlord, now dead, lived at Covent Garden, and owned many premises in Soho. I rang him immediately and he asked me to come over and see him. I laid my cards on the table and told him what part of the premises I wanted and what I wanted it for. He gave me the keys and told me to go and look the premises over first and then come back and talk business. I complied.

The rent of the whole building was something like £2,600 a year then (it would be a lot more now). I didn't have that kind of money and I told him so. Besides, I was interested only in the basement and ground floor, both of which were in a terrible condition. I told him I'd be prepared to put them in good order without any cost to him. To this he agreed and allowed me a month's rent.

Within forty-eight hours I had the building and decorating contractors on the job. I then asked Smart Alec to keep in touch with Mr de Goldini all the time and have a sharp eye on the licence; for now that I'd got the right premises I intended definitely to make it into a drinking club. I'd rather have got the licence through the proper channels if I could, yet I didn't want to lose contact with Mr de Goldini, just in case; I said *in case* because people who knew the legal aspect of drinking licences had warned me that I might not be successful with my application due to my previous prison sentences. Of course I could always put someone else with a clean record in front, but I didn't want to do that.

Anyway, I discovered that the place was going to cost me more than I'd thought. In order to raise the required sum I took a sudden plunge on a gamble that didn't come off. It was a very silly thing to do, but having developed the gambling habit it was simply one of those things which propelled one to act without sound judgement. I decided to get a financial partner, which I should have done in the first place; but then a gambler never thinks of such things. He wants all or nothing until he suddenly discovers that half a loaf would have been better than none.

I went down to the Cable Street area in the East End where

an old Nigerian friend of mine had a café. I told him about the club I was building up and its prospects, and that I wanted cash quickly. He said he had no money except his café. I asked him to sell it as quickly as possible and be my partner. Then I gave him the same line that the other fellow had given me, and took him round in a taxi to the premises immediately to let him see for himself.

He sold his business within a week and became my partner. How he settled the deal in such a short time was no concern of mine; all that mattered was that we were going to make money. Still, the bills were piling up. The basement was in a terrible condition; it had not been used for years, certainly not as a club. Toilets had to be put in, there was no end to it. We found we needed more money and neither of us could raise it. We also had to find another £75 for the licence as we had decided to buy it and open as quickly as possible without going through the police formality so that we could start earning.

We were in terrible financial straits, money, money all the time; nothing was on credit. We were paying hard cash for everything that was ordered. We had three days in which to open, invitations had already been sent out. We'd bought lots of tables and chairs but soon found out, after they were laid out, that we needed some more. The place was bigger than it looked.

That was when Smart Alec pulled his master stroke which was to net him well over £30,000 within a year.

While I was beating my brains out wondering how I was going to raise some quick money he came in with a swagger, flaunting a piece of paper in front of me.

'Well, Marke,' he said boisterously, 'that's one seventy-five pounds you don't have to worry about because I've bought the de Goldini licence myself and if you don't believe, feast your eyes on this piece of paper and read.'

When I looked I could hardly believe my own eyes; less than a couple of hours before, this man hadn't had half a crown to call his own. But another shock was to come. He flourished another piece of paper from his pocket and said confidently, 'Now read this.' It was a receipt that read: 'Received from (name) the sum of £150, £75 for tables and chairs and £75 for services rendered. Signed: W de Goldini.' He went on, 'Yes, and what's more I've bought all the tables and chairs that he had, which will fill up the corners of *our club*, and which now makes me a real partner in the business.'

I looked at the licence once more; sure enough it was genuine. I read the receipt once more. I couldn't see anything wrong with it, everything seemed to be in order with stamps and all. The only thing that puzzled me was how the hell did he raise £150 in such a short time? The receipt, I said to myself, couldn't be forged for he'd got the goods with it. I felt certain de Goldini wouldn't have parted with that licence without hard cash (he'd told me so himself), let alone his tables and chairs.

It doesn't pay to ask too many questions in Soho – besides, nothing is impossible there. I simply looked at him, shook my head in perplexity and said mildly :

' Boy, you sure must be a good hustler. Where did you raise that money so quickly?'

I didn't expect an answer and I didn't get one. He just looked at me and smiled.

' Now,' I said respectfully, ' you're the new secretary of La Boulabesse International Theatre Club' (that name was on the licence). I went on, ' The club has now removed to its new premises at 6 New Compton Street. Go now to Bow Street and notify the police regarding change of secretary and change of address.'

Thus our Smart Alec therefore became the new secretary of the club, which later changed its name to the Fulado.

From the first night of opening it was a tremendous success. Scores of coloured people and their white friends who wanted to enrol the first night couldn't get in. There was no room. They had to be told to come back some other time. We were enrolling new members at the rate of about a hundred a day and that was before the coloured GIs found out about it. When they did you couldn't keep them out if you tried.

We couldn't take money fast enough. The secretary was also the receptionist, with a couple of assistants, apart from the two stalwart men at the door. I was the floor manager. My financial partner helped behind the bar with the barmaids and was sometimes assisted by a cousin of mine with a university degree, from whom I'd borrowed some money to put in the business and who, at that time, held a responsible position at the Colonial Office. I shall just call him Herman.

On our opening night there was a little man dressed in a dinner suit helping to show members and guests to their tables. I knew he wasn't one of the waiters, yet his face seemed familiar. I asked him who he was and he replied, ' You no remember me? I am Mr de Goldini.'

I wondered why he should be helping for he had no interest in the club. But as I didn't want to embarrass him I simply said ' Oh.' However since I was concerned about his presence I sneaked into the reception hall and asked Smart Alec why Mr de Goldini was helping; did he employ him for the night without notifying me?

He replied, ' Of course not, but he's a personal friend of mine and he feels like helping. Let him if he feels that way.'

That was that and I took no more notice.

At the end of the week, at about 11.30 pm, when the club was empty except for the staff who were receiving their wages, the little man was sitting in the corner watching. I paid out the staff and left in a hurry leaving my partner and Smart Alec to settle the books. I went straight to a night club to keep an appointment and didn't get home until about 5 am.

I was just beginning to doze off when the phone rang. I looked at the little clock on the dressing table; it was just 8 am. Who could it be, I wondered, at what in night-club life is the unearthly hour of eight in the morning. I picked up the receiver. It was my financial partner speaking at the other end, but the voice was so excited I could hardly make out what he was trying to say. All I could gather was something about crooked business going on somewhere and that he was going to kill somebody.

I told him I could make neither head nor tail of his excited spiel, but if he would like to come over right away it would be okay by me.

Within half an hour he was in my flat. His story was that after I'd left the club the night before, Mr de Goldini had wanted to know why everybody was paid and nothing came to him, to which my partner replied that as far as he knew, Mr de Goldini wasn't on the payroll and he didn't know him. If he had anything to say he should have said it to me before

I left the premises. De Goldini then told him excitedly that he wasn't a servant but a partner, that he had £150 worth of shares in the business which Smart Alec had sold to him with the understanding that he would receive about £5 a week as profit which would be paid out every week from the first week of opening.

I could now see how the licence and tables and chairs had changed hands. But it was only after about two hours of patient questioning that all this became clear to me – my poor old pal was too excited to explain properly.

We left the flat about noon and went down to the club to find Smart Alec and secure an explanation from him. We didn't have to wait as he and de Goldini were already there.

The little man rushed to tell me about the affair but Smart Alec pulled him aside and told him to leave everything to him, as he could explain better. My partner then pushed Smart Alec aside and demanded that de Goldini speak for himself. Smart Alec then launched into a fight with my partner.

While I was trying to separate them, the Portuguese was pacing up and down tearing at his hair and calling upon all the gods in his quaint English, and threatening that if his partnership wasn't immediately recognized he would go straight to Bow Street police station and spill the whole basinful of beans, even if he had to spend two years in prison himself for the illegal transfer of the licence. He said he couldn't care less, because he would have the satisfaction of knowing that the lot of us would be in prison with him, and the club closed.

My poor partner must have been considering the comparative calm of his Cable Street café. Hearing this threat he went completely insane and started doing a war dance all over the club, chanting to himself and muttering that a man of his age should have known better than to invest his life blood in hard cash with a gang of West End crooks. Then he suddenly turned on me and demanded every single penny of his money back there and then – or else. He accused me of being as big a crook as Smart Alec and all the spivs in the West End. He went on to say that he never did like black men who could read and write anyway for there was no difference between them and white men. Yes, he should have known better than to go selling his good little business in the East End where he was contented and happy. He had never in his life seen even so much as the outside of a prison, let alone the inside. But, by God, if he didn't get his money before the day was over, somebody was sure to die a terrible death and he wouldn't care what happened to himself afterwards!

While he was uttering these threats, the little Portuguese was still pacing the floor and, in his turn, threatening to bring the whole of Bow Street station on Smart Alec and myself. I could do nothing but try to quieten both of them by telling them it was just a little misunderstanding that could soon be straightened out if only they would keep quiet and stop performing such antics.

It was nearly two hours later when, with the aid of my cousin who had also arrived, we brought some quiet to the club. My cousin told them if they went on that way no one would get anything except prison.

Herman and I then suggested paying back de Goldini his £150 plus interest out of the club's takings, but my cully from Cable Street would have none of that. He didn't want to have anything more to do with the club, he just wanted his money back so he could get out, and he wanted it back right now!

As he put it, 'Me no like thief business; me and thief-man nebber walk togedder, an' me no gonna start now.'

No matter how much I tried to talk him round he didn't want to know, he'd made up his mind.

I'd known him for several years. He had always treated me like a son and was an honest and straightforward man who had, as far as I knew, never gone back on his word. It broke my heart to see him so wild with me. But what could I do? I had no money to pay him off. I could easily sell his share but that would take more than a day to do, and I knew that he had such a determined mind that he'd stop at nothing when his principle was challenged. The place was like a madhouse, everybody talking at the same time; but it was Smart Alec who found the answer – as he usually did.

He called the little man aside and asked me to join them. With his slick tongue and in his most impressive manner he began, 'What's done is done and all that calling upon the gods won't help you or anybody! Now if you just keep quiet and listen to me you'll find that this is a blessing to you in disguise. This trouble is in your favour.'

De Goldini retorted, ' What you meana, favour?' Before he could say another word the weaver of words exploded:

' Just a minute my friend, don't get excited! You just listen to me! You've seen with your own eyes the kind of money this club's been taking, and we've opened only a week; within a month, when the GIs start rushing in here, the takings won't be less than four hundred pounds a day and that's talking small. This ain't the kind o' club you had in St Martin's Lane, and you bloody know it! This is your chance to buy that man's partnership. All he wants is the money he put in, not a penny more! You heard him say so yourself. Now just you listen, I could walk out of here now and be back within two hours with a man who would be quick to give me double the money that silly ole so-and-so wants, and I could pay him off and still get at least 250 pounds over. I could then pay you off too for your tables, chairs and licence, and I'd still be in pocket. Mr Marke knows the man I'm talking about, he'd offer any amount of money for a partnership in this business but Marke and I don't like him, that's all.' He turned to look at me. ' Isn't that so, Marke?'

I nodded, although I hadn't the faintest idea to whom he was referring.

He went on, ' But we won't do that except if we have to. We are going to give you the first chance, all because I've known you a long time and we are friends. Now I know you have the money and consider yourself very lucky. Give this mug a cheque for exactly what he put in, and you are a full partner. There are witnesses, and we can draw up the agreement later.'

The Portuguese was so pleased he couldn't pull out his cheque book quick enough. My ill-used friend demanded an open cheque which he intended cashing promptly on Monday. There had been no written agreement between us so nothing in writing was required. But before he left he made it quite clear that since he couldn't read, if he found there had been any monkeying and the bank wouldn't honour the cheque he'd be right back and it would be just too bad for the little man.

To make his point, he walked back to de Goldini, gave him a severe slap on the face and then stormed out.

I was glad my old pal didn't have to return. After he left I felt lonely and downcast. For him to think that I was in a swindle against him was something I couldn't bear. I went two or three times to the East End to see him and explain, but he refused to discuss anything with me. This gave me no peace of mind and caused me nights of restless sleep. Finally I asked the Portuguese to buy my share. But this he wouldn't do though I had the feeling he had the money. Smart Alec, who didn't want me to leave, tried for days to talk me out of it. But I too had made up my mind.

I knew this would mean financial retrogression. But since I'd decided to leave, nothing in the world could prevent me from doing so. I have never wanted to be a millionaire; money to me has always been for what it is worth. And I knew that as long as I retained my health I could always make it elsewhere – where I would be happy and not have an old friend's disillusionment on my conscience. I knew full well that if I became weak and failed to bring my partnership to an end, my old friend would never believe that I had no part in Smart Alec's trickery.

In fairness to Smart Alec, when he found out that I was determined to leave, he called me aside and said in a serious tone, 'Listen, Marke, you're making the biggest financial mistake in your life by leaving this business and you'll regret it. Because that old mug is ignorant and stupid enough to walk out of a progressive business is no reason why you should do the same.'

I could have told him that there was a little thing called principle. But I would have been wasting my breath. There is only one thing that fellows of that kidney know, and that is the big and mighty £sd.

This Smart Alec was right and yet he was wrong. He was right when he said I was making the biggest financial mistake in my life. But he wasn't telling me anything I didn't already know. For a second-rate club the Fulado made more money than any club of its kind in England, and I had expected it. He was wrong when he said that I would regret it. I would never regret anything I'd done, for it is through trial and errors that we gain experience. Besides, I am a strong believer in the proverb: 'What will be will be.' Perhaps it is for this reason I have always been able to face disappointment.

As I had expected, the little Portuguese's partnership in the business was short lived. Smart Alec saw to that! Yet he made a good profit the short time he was there – within two years the twister was a rich man. He became a notable figure on the dogtrack. He bought and owned racing dogs and became the owner of one of the fastest dogs in the country. But like most ill-gotten gains he lost it all and had to leave Britain in a hurry – for his health. I bear him no malice. He did nothing that hadn't been done before in high circles. In Soho they call it plain hustling.

Soon after I terminated my partnership at the Fulado Club I found myself in another unpleasant situation. I had boarded a bus on my way to Wardour Street to complete a deal with an estate agent over the lease of 5 Gerrard Street, which I intended using as a social club; on opening my newspaper I saw a report which read something like this:

'Two people were shot in front of the Tatler Theatre, Charing Cross Road, about eleven o'clock last night. A coloured man is suspected.'

I stopped reading, jumped off the bus at the next stop and hailed a cruising taxi back to my flat in order to put away the gun which I had in my pocket. For I knew only too well that I would be one of the first coloured men to be picked up for questioning, and naturally I couldn't afford this to happen with a loaded gun on my person. I was innocent and had an alibi. But I knew I would have been in trouble for having the gun, and I just couldn't afford to go to jail then – not with this business deal on my hands.

I hid the gun in the folds of one of my laundered shirts in a drawer, went out again and finished the deal. Then I strolled down for a drink at the Fulado Club in New Compton Street. I wasn't there ten minutes when I was tapped on the shoulder by a detective sergeant whom I knew. He was with another detective.

'The chief wants to see you, Ernest,' he said placidly, 'Come on.'

I was quietly escorted outside and into a car. And soon we were at Vine Street police station.

The chief superintendent was at his desk and appeared to be studying a photograph. He came straight to the point. 'Why do you carry a gun?'

'I don't carry a gun any more,' I lied. 'You can search me.'

He looked closely at me for a moment. Then he shook his head. 'Do you mind your premises being searched?'

'No,' I stammered and thought, what a question! – as if I could object. I then regretted going back home with the gun. But then there was no way of my knowing I wouldn't be searched.

He showed me the picture on the desk. It was of a dead man of Latin origin with two bullet wounds on his naked chest. 'This man wasn't even British,' he said mildly. 'But we still got the murderer – an Englishman. So don't think you were brought here simply because you are coloured.'

He looked at the detectives. 'Okay, take him to his premises, search them and bring him back.'

All the way to the flat my heart was beating furiously, hoping against hope that they wouldn't find the gun. But they did.

The detective sergeant looked at me solemnly. 'I thought you told the chief you haven't got a gun?'

'I told him I don't carry a gun any more,' I retorted. 'That was the truth, wasn't it? This gun is found on my premises, not on my person. You didn't expect me to tell him I had a gun indoors, did you?' I had to say something in defence.

He looked solemnly at me. 'Neither did he. This doesn't look too good, does it? Okay, let's go.'

When I was questioned at the station I told everything except the part where I did have the gun on my person earlier in the bus. I remembered exactly where I was the night before at the time of the shooting. So apart from the offence of possessing a revolver and ammunition without a licence, which was bad enough with my record, I was certain I couldn't be charged with the shooting for I had a perfect alibi from 8 pm to 11.15 pm. And because I was so accurate regarding the time, the superintendent became suspicious and asked me how I remembered the time in question so accurately. I then made the following statement:

'I was away on a visit to my family in Manchester. I arrived back at Euston just after six pm yesterday. I couldn't help seeing the clock in front of me as I came off the train. I went home, had a wash and a change and then went straight to my favourite club, the Caribbean in Denman Street. I couldn't say what time I arrived there but it must have been before eight pm. I know this because an artiste friend of mine, a dancer by the name of Slim Isaac, was in the club. I joined his company. And after a couple of drinks he suddenly stood to his feet and said he had to leave as he had an appointment at eight o'clock at Leicester Square. I looked at my watch and told him it was eight ten and by the time he got to Leicester Square it was bound to be at least eight twenty.

'I then asked jokingly if the appointment was a dame, to which he replied yes. I said, laughing, that no respectable dame was going to wait twenty minutes on a street corner for a man, especially when the man was no Ali Khan. I slapped him on the back and urged him to sit down and drink with me and forget the date. We drank together the rest of the evening and I never left the premises till well after eleven o'clock.'

I was detained for further questioning. And though I did not know it then, my alibi was being checked. The receptionist and the proprietor of the club and even the barmaids were questioned over and over again about the exact time I left the premises. They were even asked how they could be so sure, with a well-filled club like that, of the exact time that I left. They truthfully replied that it was a habit of mine to be one of the last to leave the club every night and the night in question was no exception.

The police also visited my dancer friend at his home in Maida Vale, and he confirmed my story. I was then let out on my own bail to appear at Marlborough Street police court on the next morning on the charge of possessing a gun and ammunition without a permit.

I appeared before the late Mr Sandbach the next morning and pleaded guilty to the charge. My record was read out. I didn't expect anything less than a term of imprisonment but

Mr Sandbach didn't send me to prison, much to my surprise. Instead he asked,

'Why do you have to possess a gun?'

I then told him all about the incident at Great Windmill Street. I added that before that I hadn't carried one for a long time as I'd made a pledge to myself never to do so again after my last trouble. I didn't ask for a chance as I'd never expected any and didn't think I'd get it. But if there ever was a godly and understanding magistrate, it was Mr Sandbach.

He listened attentively to me till I finished, then he made a short speech which I can't recall word for word, but it was something like this:

'I have no reason to disbelieve your story. There are certain elements around who think that because a person is of a different colour or race he should not be allowed to share the same social rights. Until such people wake up and come to their senses the world will never be at peace. I am going to take the law into my own hands and do what I really shouldn't do, that is not send you to prison, which you deserve, simply because I believe your story.' He went on, 'But don't minimize the situation. Carrying loaded guns around is not allowed in this country and we are not going to tolerate it. Don't let me see you here again on that charge. Pay twenty pounds.'

I had stopped crying since I was a lad. But I walked out of that courtroom with an emotional lump in my throat, a tear drop on my cheek. I went home and there on my bended knees I thanked God for creating men like Mr Sandbach, and promised myself I'd never carry or keep another gun.

I haven't carried another gun since and have no intention of doing so.

Prior to my taking the lease of the Gerrard Street premises, not being one to sit around doing nothing, I had gone back at my old job at the Brewer Street club owned by Harry Etting.

One evening two CID men called at the club and asked me if I knew a girl called Iris . . . to which I replied yes. They then wanted to know when was the last time I saw her. I told them truthfully that I could not remember, but it was a matter of weeks. They gave me the names of two men who they said were GIs. But I never took much interest in names –

especially where Yanks were concerned. To me they were just GIs and I told them so. I was then told that they had reason to believe that I knew these particular GIs and knew about their recent activities, so I'd better come clean for this was a serious matter; the sooner Iris and the GIs were apprehended the better.

I had no idea what they were talking about, and I said so. They went on to tell me these three were wanted for stick-up jobs. And this might lead to murder if they were not apprehended in time.

'Why should I know anything about them?' I said indignantly. 'I'm no angel and never have been, but my business is gambling when I'm not on the roads; why pick on me?' I added, 'I've never been a stick-up merchant in my life, and I don't know anyone who is.'

After listening to them for a while it suddenly dawned on me who these two GIs could be. I'd absolutely forgotten about them; in any case it had never occurred to me that the Iris I knew could have had anything to do with a stick-up merchant. Iris was a well-educated Jewish girl from a wonderful home and God-fearing family. Now that I'd recollected, everything came to mind. I then recounted the following incidents: I was stopped one evening at Charing Cross Road by two young coloured GIs who asked me to show them the rounds. This I refused. But I told them I was on my way to a club frequented by coloured people and GIs. And if they cared to come with me I could sign them in and they might meet some of their buddies there.

We went to the club and I found them to be well-behaved, so when I was going to another club and they asked if they could come with me, I allowed them. In the next club I met Iris whom I'd known for a while. I introduced them, and Iris joined our company. About 10.30 pm I left them with Iris as I had to go to work.

The next day about 1 pm I was still in bed as I'd been working late and didn't get home till about eight in the morning. I heard the bell ring and when I opened the door it turned out to be Iris and the two Yanks. I wasn't surprised, for nothing like that surprised me in the West End. I led them to the sitting room, pointed out the cocktail cabinet and told them to help themselves to drinks while I got dressed.

We drank together the whole afternoon then I told them to excuse me as I had to go out. We all went out together and parted company in the West End. The next day the lads came back to see me, and the day after; I didn't mind in the least, they seemed to be nice boys and were rather amusing. Then they told me that they were on leave and had run short of money but didn't want to return to camp yet as their leave wasn't over. They didn't want to borrow any money; they only wanted to know if I could do them a little favour by letting them stay with me till their leave expired. They still had a little spending money left but not enough for hotel bills. They promised not to be in the way and said they would leave the flat every evening when I went out for the night, and would then hang around the all-night cafés till morning, waiting till I got back home; then they would be quite satisfied to have a few hours' nap in the sitting room.

I saw nothing wrong with this arrangement since I was living alone and thought they would be good company. More often than not I would meet them sitting on the doorstep on my arrival. They made themselves useful by cleaning the flat and doing most of the shopping for me. I did the cooking as usual for I pride myself on that. For their services I sometimes gave them a pound or two in the evenings when they were going out and told them to have a drink on me.

After about six days of this and nothing said about going back to camp I began to get suspicious, so on the seventh day I asked them how long their leave was. They told me it was a month. This made me more suspicious as I'd never heard of a GI having a month's leave yet in this country and I said so. But when they retorted, ' Man we get a month's leave all the time,' I had to accept it, for after all I knew nothing about GIs and their leaves. However I decided they'd have to go since I had no intention of harbouring any deserters and getting myself into trouble, as if I hadn't enough troubles of my own. And since it wasn't easy for me to tell them they had to go, because I had come to like them for the amusing stories they often told, I had to put it tenderly and in their own idiom.

' Listen here fellers. I ain't saying you fellers ain't got a month's leave 'cause I don't think you all going lie to me anyway, but I don't know how long you been on leave before I met you. You guys being GIS, and me being a civilian, if it happens that you got mixed up on your leave I'm liable to catch it plenty! See what I mean? That's law to us civilians! Now I know you guys wouldn't like to see me in trouble, especially since I got a good job, which I sure would lose if I get sent to jail see? So what about going back to camp tomorrow? 'Course, if you don't wanna go back there ain't nothing I can do about it. But just the same you find some place else, see? You can come up and see me any time you like and eat and drink with me, so long as you don't come too often, that way I ain't in no spot with the law, see what I mean?'

They took it calmly. And after they left the flat that evening I never saw them again, nor did I see anything of Iris after the day she brought the men to my flat. That's why I couldn't connect the three at first.

After I had narrated these facts I added that since then I had met a number of coloured GIS in clubs, drunk with them and sometimes invited them home for more drinks and company. And never would I remember their names. Before the officers left I was told that if I should remember anything else or happen to see them I must ring the station at once. They left their telephone number. But I was glad I didn't have to do so, for that same night, as I was later informed, the three were picked up somewhere in Piccadilly.

The two lads were tried by an American court and given five years. Iris was put away for three years in Borstal or some place like that. She was only young herself. They were lucky to be picked up in time or Iris might have ended up like Betty Jones in the Cleft Chin murder case: this girl had teamed up with an American deserter in a course of robbery at gun point, which led to murder.

It so happened after I'd told the lads to go, since they had no money apart from what I'd given them and were deserters as I'd suspected, they met Iris again; they became good friends with her and arranged with her to lure men into back streets while they relieved them of their wallets at gun point. Iris was indeed a strange girl.

It wasn't long after the CID men came to see me about Iris that I opened the Coloured Colonial Social Club at 5 Gerrard

Street. An interest in furthering the welfare of my fellow black men had always been with me, ever since the race riot of 1919 which I described earlier. In fact, just after I was medically discharged from the merchant navy where I'd served my call-up, I started an organization which I named the Coloured Workers' Association – now dissolved. This association is not to be confused with the present one of the same name, which was formed years later. We used to have our meetings regularly in the big front room on the first floor of the club premises. Many African big names of today in the political field had attended the meetings, including the late Dr Kwame Nkrumah, who often acted as the chairman. He had just arrived from the United States where he had been a student.

I think Nkrumah was the greatest African I ever had the pleasure of knowing – if for no other reason than that he started the wind of change in Africa. I am also proud to have known Jomo Kenyatta, now President of Kenya. We first met in the early thirties when filming *Sanders of the River* with Paul Robeson. I was an extra, and Jomo took the part of one of the tribal chiefs. No one then, including himself, would have dreamt that he was destined to become the liberator and president of his country.

Many years later in Manchester we met again and became acquainted through a mutual friend, Mr Makonen, a well known Manchester restaurateur and politician. We then went about together a couple of times. He had a very strong personality, though quiet and unassuming.

Both he, Nkrumah and myself attended the first Pan-African Conference, which took place in the middle forties at All Saints, Manchester. Dr Dubois, the eminent American negro educationalist, was in the chair. It was at this conference that Nkrumah proclaimed loud and clear that when the Gold Coast became independent it would henceforth be known as Ghana. The reason he gave for this was that the people who were now settled in the Gold Coast had emigrated from somewhere in North West Africa, the name of which was Ghana.

It was soon after this conference that Nkrumah went back to the Gold Coast and formed the Convention People's Party. Soon he was sent to prison, daubed as a dangerous agitator by the British. And the people went raving mad. The authorities soon rectified their mistake and released him – only to install him as the first prime minister of the Gold Coast.

The Coloured Workers' Association itself was a relatively short-lived affair. Possibly the climate wasn't yet ready for the organized societies we see today, and in any event there were too many people with contradictory aims within it. But I like to think, perhaps a little fancifully, that within that organization a small breeze of independence sprang up, which years later became the 'wind of change.'

Besides, having always been as much of a businessman as a political campaigner, I gave more of my energy to my clubs than to the cause of African independence. Thus the Coloured Colonial Social Club was opened; I did not find the running of it uneventful.

It was about nine o'clock in the morning. I was just trying to have some sleep after being on business all night, when the phone rang. On the other end of the line was a strange voice.

'This is Detective Inspector Black ringing from your club premises at Gerrard Street . . . Please come over right away . . . it's important. Your doorman is with me and I'm waiting for you.'

In that line of business a call like this was never surprising, but they made one uneasy. Detective Inspector Black was from the murder squad. So on my way to meet him I started searching my brain to remember all the places I could have been within the last week or so – an alibi is always essential.

When I arrived, the inspector was with another detective, together with my doorman, who slept on the premises. I didn't have to look at the doorman's face twice to know that whatever it was, it must be serious.

The inspector introduced himself and the other detective and asked mildly, 'When did you last see Philip Berry?'

'Philip Berry? I'm afraid, inspector, I don't know who you mean.'

He looked me squarely in the eye while his colleague searched my face.

'Are you sure you don't know who I mean?' he asked suspiciously.

'Sure I'm sure, inspector, never heard of that name before,' I answered.

'Now,' he said seriously, 'think well before you answer the next question. First I must tell you that we have reason to believe that Philip Berry was in these premises in the early hours of the morning; for how long we don't know, but we know he was here. Concealing any knowledge of this man will get you into serious trouble and I'm sure you don't want that. Philip Berry is wanted for murder. Now, what time was Philip Berry here?'

'I still don't know who you're talking about, Inspector,' I said. 'But I do know that I've never heard of that name before. If it was registered in my books I would remember, for I personally register every member in this club. I'll show you the books and you can see for yourself.'

I asked the doorman to bring me the books and added, 'Of course, he might have been here with somebody; but I can assure you, Inspector, there was no strange face here last night, nor this morning for that matter. If there were I would have noticed it, for I never left the premises till after six this morning. I was the last man to leave the premises apart from the doorman who sleeps here.'

The books were brought and examined by the inspector and myself. Just as I had said, there was no such name as Philip Berry in the books.

'Now you see what I mean, Inspector,' I said with relief.

The inspector placed his hand in his pocket and produced a photograph.

'Do you know this man?'

I looked at the picture. 'That's Creeping Jesus!' I exclaimed. 'Sure I know him.'

'Well,' said the inspector. 'This is Philip Berry. What time was he here this morning?'

'About one o'clock this morning,' I said, 'He was here till six. I had to throw him out when I wanted to close up as he didn't want to go.' I stammered, 'B... But are you sure that's the man you want?'

I just couldn't believe it; you could have cut my legs and called me shorty. Not that Philip Berry wasn't capable of murder. He'd only just come out of jail for the attempted murder of his wife, but it was his cool action just after the murder had been committed that made me doubt it, and I thought there was a mistake somewhere.

I saw him just before 1 am when he walked into the billiard room, faced two fellows who were playing a game of billiards, and said, ' I challenge the winner of this game.'

I went straight up to him and told him he wasn't challenging anybody in this game or any other game, and ordered him to leave the premises immediately.

I'd already barred him from the premises days before after he was accused of stealing money from a member. He had never been a member of the club and I wouldn't have made him one if he'd cried his eyes out, simply because he had a creepy way about him that gave me the shivers. One could never hear his footsteps; you just felt that somebody was behind you and when you looked round he'd be standing there grinning at you. He had a habit of walking just like a ghost, or at least as I imagined a ghost would walk. I didn't even know how he got in the club; I asked the doorman, who'd had strict orders about him. And he didn't know.

After I'd ordered him to leave he started pleading and turned his pockets inside out, saying that he was broke.

' Ah can't go 'ome till the toobs start 'cause Ah got no money fo' taxi. Ah promise Ah no trouble nobody. Please let me stay only till toob or bus start.' All he had was a shilling. And since his expression was rather pathetic I had to let him stay.

' But,' I said aggressively, ' this is the last time you ever pass through these doors.' Then on second thoughts I added, ' or through these windows, or whatever way you came in.'

I went back upstairs to the card room where I joined a game of poker till about 5.30 am. By six o'clock everybody had left the premises except Creeping Jesus, whom I found stretched out on two chairs, snoring in front of the fire in the billiard room downstairs. He was so deep in sleep that it took me well over two minutes to wake him up, and even then he was still half asleep and refused to leave. He wanted to stay a little longer as he said he was very tired. I then lost patience with him and dragged him out and shut the door. He was still half asleep.

Now how could I believe that a man acting like that had

only just killed a man by shooting him through the heart and firing more bullets at the body to make sure he was dead, then walked straight to a club, made himself comfortable and slept peacefully for the rest of the night. It just didn't make sense and I told the inspector so.

He replied, ' Just the same, he's wanted for murder.'

When Philip Berry was arrested a couple of hours later in Camden Town, had he not readily confessed to the murder I would never have believed it, for I would have thought without any doubt that it was a case of mistaken identity. Every time I think of the way I manhandled Creeping Jesus that morning a cold chill runs up my spine.

It was about 11.30 pm. The pubs at Kings Cross had all closed. A small bespectacled negro walked to a coffee stand opposite St Pancras station and ordered a cup of coffee. He moved the coffee to a corner of the bar and started sipping it. At the opposite corner was another negro in an American uniform also having coffee – with a white woman. A few white people were standing in front of the bar chatting and drinking tea.

A big six foot four inches tall white man staggered to the bar. Those in front of the bar moved to make room for him. The atmosphere became tense amongst the white customers for most of them knew this man to be a bully and a quarrelsome person when he'd had some drinks, and it was obvious that he'd had plenty which was not unusual.

The man suddenly spotted the GI and his white woman friend. He pushed his way to him aggressively.

' You black bastard, where you come from you daren't look at a white woman let alone eat with her.'

The GI pretended not to take any notice of him, but the man collared him and tried to pull him out. A fight then developed between the two. The bystanders intervened and stopped the fight. The white woman then began to lead the GI towards the American hostel for negro GIS around the corner.

The bully suddenly dashed back towards them, pulled the white woman away and again attacked the negro. The negro didn't seem to be a match for this huge broad-shouldered man.

This was too much for Philip Berry who was sipping his coffee in the corner, unnoticed and watching; for it turned out that the little bespectacled negro was none other than Philip Berry, better known as Creeping Jesus or the Creeper.

Philip then left his corner and walked straight towards the two. He tapped the big man on the back and told him to lay off the GI. Naturally when the big bully looked round and saw that it was another nigger and a little one at that, he lifted his hand to hit Berry – but that was the last thing he ever did.

Berry pulled out a gun and shot him stone dead with the first bullet. Then as the man lay dead on the ground, he shot a few more bullets into his body just to make sure.

He then walked through Euston Road, down Tottenham Court Road and Charing Cross Road, then right into Shaftesbury Avenue, left to Gerrard's Place and then right to Gerrard Street and my club. That's how he led the police to my club.

After listening to the preliminary hearing at Clerkenwell magistrates' court I went to Brixton prison, where he was remanded, to see him and to see if there was anything I could do for him. With me I took Mr Yallah, a countryman of his from Nigeria, thinking that if he wouldn't talk to me he would talk to Yallah.

But all he said was, 'Mr Marke, you can't do not'in' fo' me, nobody can! T'ank you jus' same. If Ah get chance to do same t'ing again, Ah'll do it! Dat man him was no good!'

I told Yallah to talk to him in their own language, but even to Yallah he said nothing more than what he'd told me. He was sentenced to death.

I felt so moved about this that I started a lecture tour in coloured clubs, which took me among other places to Cardiff, Liverpool and Manchester in order to raise funds for an appeal. I only collected a mere pittance which with a little of my own money I handed over to the committee of coloured people, which had been set up for this purpose.

Philip Berry was later reprieved, thanks to a brilliant KC. But he didn't live long after his release and died tragically.

Walking along Soho Square on my way to the Jungle Club in Frith Street one evening I came across him and stopped to hand him a couple of bob. Less than half an hour later a coloured man came to the club and announced that the Creeper had just died. He had dropped dead at a bus stop in Oxford Street a few minutes after seeing me.

Mr Ola Dosumu, the Nigerian who once owned the old Abalabi Club in Berwick Street and later owned the more elite Club Afrique in Wardour Street, took charge of his funeral. He owned a few houses and usually looked after his own countrymen when they were broke and had nowhere to go, and he had done so for the Creeper when he came out of jail.

The least I could do was to take the Creeper a wreath. Though I never did like Philip Berry I came to respect him and shall always remember him. A man who would lay down his life to defend the rights of a total stranger wasn't one to be disrespected.

It was soon after the Philip Berry incident and Germany had just surrendered. I was in my office just after 11 pm when I heard an unusual bang from the ground floor. I rushed downstairs to see what it was all about and a brick whizzed an inch wide of my head and landed on the stairway. The front door facing the stairway was wide open and outside in the street were about half a dozen white men in American uniforms, shouting and demonstrating. I rushed to the door and bolted it. Then I looked into the billiard room. The few men inside, all of whom were coloured, were absolutely terrified.

I rushed back up to the first floor, switched off the light in the front room and peeped through the curtains, only to see more uniformed Americans coming from around the corner at Gerrard Place to join their colleagues. Those in front of the building were gesticulating, swearing and shouting, 'Break down the goddamn door . . .' 'Get the niggers out.'

And still there were more GIs coming from round the corner.

It didn't occur to me to ring for the police though I had a phone in my office; the only thing that entered my mind then was to fight back and protect my premises. As there were about twenty coloured people altogether in the club, I decided that Ola Dusumo – who was then my chief croupier – and I should organize them.

The mob was now banging at the door and making furious noises.

The first thing Ola and I did was to assure the men in the club that there was nothing to be afraid of, for some of them were now in a state of panic and I was apprehensive lest the rest become infected. If they did we'd have had it.

One fellow had already jumped through one of the back windows, as we found out later, but he didn't get far. He found himself right in the middle of a gang of GIs in Shaftesbury Avenue, on their way from the Rainbow Corner, an American hostel nearby, to join forces with their friends. They nearly murdered him.

While I was organizing the men on the ground floor, Ola was gathering the rest of the men who had run up to the top floors seeking ways of escape. He shepherded the lot downstairs. By the time they reached the ground floor we were busy filling up every empty bottle with water and lining them in the hallway. After everyone had made sure he was holding a bottle or two, Ola then took command.

These actions were performed a lot quicker than it takes to put into words. By this time the mob was trying to ram the door open.

We lined ourselves up in the hallway, Ola in front, I behind him and the rest behind me. Ola then released the bolt. As the door flew open those who fell in were immediately dealt with, while the rest of us rushed out and started lashing at the others. This sudden move seemed to surprise them and they became confused. We battered the daylights out of those we could handle. Within one minute we were back in with the door closed, getting ready for the next assault.

By the time we were ready to repeat it we heard the report of a gun but no sign of a bullet through the door. (I learned later that the gun was fired in the air by an American MP trying to quell the mob.) Then a sudden quietness, followed by a loud knock on the door. ' Okay, it's the police,' said a voice in an English accent. ' Open up.'

Cautiously we opened the door, bottles in hand in case it was a trick. Facing us were a number of civil policemen and behind them a number of American military police with drawn guns.

They then shepherded us into the waiting van, assuring us it was for our own protection, leaving some officers behind to guard the premises.

Soon we were at West End Central police station. I was led

to a desk and asked to make a statement. An hour or two later an American sailor, head heavily bandaged and face plastered, was brought in by a couple of MPs to identify the man who had caused his injury.

We were all lined up for the identification but he couldn't pick out anyone. Had he done so he would have been a liar, for it would have been impossible for anyone to identify any single individual in that one short skirmish in the dark. It was a question of coloured men in civilian clothes versus white men in American uniform.

Many Yanks were hurt, but apart from the frightened coloured man who made his escape only to fall in the hands of the GIs none of us had even a scratch.

The attack was absolutely unprovoked. In the first place, with the exception of three GIs, two coloured and one white who were personal friends of mine, I wouldn't entertain any American, white or black. So I had named the club the Coloured Colonial Social Club, which was painted boldly outside the club premises. It was part of my policy.

The reason for this was that though the Yanks were the best customers at the Fulado Club and spent their money wildly some of them were dangerous customers who had drawn guns amongst themselves more than once. Razor and knife fights were common amongst them and on more than one occasion the military police had to be called in. However the Fulado Club was licensed whereas the Coloured Colonial Club wasn't. Provided this type of club was run in a well-conducted manner, the police would turn a blind eye to the illegal gaming which often went on so they could keep a sharp eye on the criminals who often visited such places to gamble their ill-gotten gains. Every three months or so there would be a police raid and a fine or short prison sentence imposed on the owners. But the moment a gun, razor or knife fight took place the club would automatically be closed and no amount of influence or money could open it again. My long years of experience in running this type of club have taught me this. And since I had no intention whatever of being tempted by the easy American money and getting my business closed I had to be careful whom I let in.

Because this full-scale unprovoked attack took place less than a week after the end of the war it frightened me and also made me furious, for in my mind's eye I could clearly see the 1919 race riot repeating itself, with the victorious white race making whoopee at the expense and misery of the black race which had helped him to defeat his common enemy.

I voiced my opinion at the police station. The superintendent in charge, whose name I cannot recall, asked me not to take it that way for it had been just the action of some irresponsible Americans. I couldn't see it that way, at least not at that time. I told him so, and added,

'I shall advise every coloured man I know, and I know plenty, to carry loaded guns, knives and razors on their person from now on.'

He replied, 'I know just how you feel but take my advice and get that idea out of your head right now.' He added, 'Such action will only worsen the situation and make it harder for the police. You can rest assured that the police will do all in their power to handle the situation.' He stopped for a moment, eyed me and went on, 'If you want to help, the least you can do is to discourage weapon-carrying amongst your people instead of encouraging it. Open your club as usual and tell your men to keep off the streets and leave the rest to us.'

It was 9 am when I left the police station. I rang Mr Ivor Cummings, OBE, of the Colonial Office Welfare Department, to tell him of the trouble. He already knew all about it because it was front-page news in all the papers – with pictures to match. He asked me to come over right away and see him.

I didn't lose any time getting to the office which was then in Park Street, Mayfair. There wasn't much to tell, everything had started so suddenly and finished so quickly. But he listened attentively to what little I had to say. Then he told me not to worry as the authorities would soon have the situation in hand. It turned out to be sooner than I'd expeced.

I thanked him and got up to leave. But he must have sensed something for he stretched out a hand and touched mine. 'Now listen, before you go I must warn you. Don't carry firearms or offensive weapons, and do all in your power to see that the rest of your associates don't. We don't want the situation to get out of hand. Do you promise?'

I promised and left.

Reaching home I went straight to bed. But sleep was impossible. The race riot which took place immediately after the First World War kept flaring in front of me. I stayed indoors till about 8 pm, then I decided to go back to the club and open up as the superintendent had advised.

Coming to Gerrard Street my jaws dropped when I saw the squad of armed American military and naval police, assisted by the civil police, patrolling the street. And now the whole street was out of bounds to American service men.

I opened up the club, immediately rang a few associates and told them to flash the news around that the club was open again, and better still it was now well protected by the British civil police and the American MPs; there was nothing to be afraid of as the whole street was out of bounds to American servicemen. But under no circumstances must anyone carry an offensive weapon of any kind. I also let it be known that they were liable to be searched by the civil police, and if any weapon was found it would mean prison.

The news went around all right but only a few braved it and came to the club that night and the night after. But when the rest were assured that everything was on the level and they could indeed play poker and shoot dice as much as they liked without being raided, in no time the club began to fill up again. But now the number of members had been multiplied. Everybody wanted to be a member all of a sudden.

For nearly a month Gerrard Street was well guarded night and day, during which time the games went on and on. Never in the whole gaming history of Great Britain had so many black gamblers had it so good, and never have I made so much money in so short a time. Black faces were coming from far and wide to the Coloured Colonial Club to play the illegal games of dice and poker, lawfully, under the watchful eyes of the two greatest authorities in the West. This is not likely to happen again in my or anybody else's lifetime.

8

THE END OF THE ROAD

All good things must come to an end. Early in 1946, long after the American MPs and British civil police had been called off, I was sitting in my office one evening doing my books when Dudley, my doorman, came up and told me that a gentleman was waiting in the hallway on the ground floor, wanting to see me. Without lifting my eyes from what I was doing I told Dudley to send the man up.

The visitor turned out to be Gentleman Jim, who wasn't a gentleman at all and whose name I didn't think was Jim; he was so called because he always wore a bowler hat and carried a rolled umbrella, and his trousers were always pressed sharp even if they were a bit greasy. His real name I didn't know.

I raised my eyes from what I was doing and there was Jim looking down at me with his piggy eyes, and a forced smile on his wrinkled face. I was rather surprised to see the man, not only because he was no associate of mine but he wasn't even a member of my club for the simple reason that he wasn't a gambler at all; he was a con man whom I had often seen in drinking clubs, with a glass of whisky in his hand and his shifty eyes weighing up everybody. I wondered. And because I knew that he hadn't come to put me on a 'good thing,' since he knew that I knew what he was and naturally he must know that I wouldn't fall for any of his lines, I became apprehensive. All this 'knew' and 'know' must sound like a cloak-and-dagger affair, but any club proprietor who runs an illegal business on his premises and hasn't the slightest idea of the workings of a criminal mind might just as well pack it up. And that also goes for the crook who may want to pull the wool over the proprietor's eyes.

After all, it's a well-known fact that most of the customers or members in these places were either professional or part-time crooks. It was for this reason – before the present Gaming Act was passed – that the police were never inclined to close these premises, for they were convenient to them when searching for wanted criminals. I was apprehensive because in that line of business when one was not busy trying to outwit a police raid, which was sure to come sooner or later, one would be busy trying to avoid getting entangled in the criminal's web.

'Hello, Marke,' Jim said, and he drew himself up a chair. Though we'd never spoken to each other before, I wasn't surprised that he knew my name; in that circle nearly everyone knew each other and knew what he did for a living even if they had never spoken to each other before.

'What can I do for you, Mr Jim?' I said.

He pulled out two cigars from his waistcoat pocket, handed me one, bit off the end of the other and stuck it in his mouth; I had a feeling he was weighing me up all the time.

Pulling a box of matches from the pocket of his trench coat he took out one match and waited for me to put my cigar in my mouth. After lighting my cigar he lit his own, blew out the flame and carefully placed the stick in the ashtray on my desk. He took his eyes away from me and puffed a ring of smoke in the air.

He turned his eyes towards me again. 'I heard that you've had trouble with the Yanks. They tried to break up your place, I believe.'

I wondered what this was leading up to.

'I was away at the time,' Jimmy said (as if I didn't know he'd been a compulsory guest at one of His Majesty's guest houses and had just been released). 'Got back last week. And yesterday, while I was drinking with Tommy Donnelly – you know Donnelly, don't you?' (The name Donnelly is fictitious.)

'Never heard of him,' I said. Acting unconcerned I threw my head back and blew out circles of smoke towards the ceiling.

'Never heard of Tommy Donnelly?' he asked with crinkled brow. 'Why, anyone who is anyone around here knows Donnelly. The man's got a reputation. But then perhaps you've not been going around lately.'

'Not been going around lately!' I thought. 'I, who do the rounds every night from seven to eleven, and sometimes up till four in the morning – posh clubs, low clubs, clip joints, the lot!' I smiled faintly. 'Perhaps,' I said. 'What's the message?'

For a moment he didn't answer. He looked towards the ceiling and puffed hard at his cigar while I eyed him impatiently.

'Well, what is it, Mr Jim?' I asked nervously without making it obvious.

'Well,' he said, 'while I was drinking with Tommy Don – ...' He stopped suddenly and lowered his eyes. Then he looked straight into mine. 'You know, Marke, I may be able to do you a favour,' he said coldly.

'What kind of a favour?' I asked quietly, but suspiciously.

Jimmy said, 'You may not know who Tommy Donnelly is but I can tell you he is a straightforward man who wouldn't stand any nonsense from people who take liberties with club proprietors. He believes that running a club is a hard enough graft without liberty takers and layabouts causing trouble. And he's bloody right, don't you agree?'

I didn't make any comment, but now that I knew what he was leading up to I was wondering what treatment I should give him.

He went on, 'Donnelly has formed an organization which protects all club proprietors around this area. He intends to put a stop to all this messing about...'

I raised my eyebrows, but kept silent.

'In fact, Donnelly told me yesterday that though you haven't yet joined the organization, had he known about those Yanks he would've been here with his mob and settled them good and proper! And believe me he would've done it. You may not know this, Marke, but Donnelly and his men don't do things in half measures. They can be real tearaways when the occasion arises...'

This sounded like a threat, and having a hot temper I had to stop myself exploding by gripping the edge of the desk tightly.

Jimmy went on, 'Nobody takes liberties with Donnelly and the people he protects...'

'That may be so, Mr Jim,' I interrupted, 'but please come to the point. What has all this got to do with me?'

He shrugged his shoulders, expanded his arms and pushed his face forward. 'Sure, you're not a mug, Marke, or you wouldn't be in this business. In fact all the clever proprietors around here have already joined the organization; it only costs a few pounds a week and it saves a lot of trouble. I thought perhaps you didn't know about it. That's why I'm here – see what I mean?'

I felt like attacking him. But I controlled myself. 'Look, Mr Jim,' I said coldly, 'during the Yankee incident I had the greatest protection any man could hope for, even though my members and I are black. Maybe Tommy Donnelly didn't tell you that. In any case what makes you think that this guy and his mob can do better than the police?'

'That's not the point,' he said. 'You were just lucky at that time. You know as well as I do that the coppers are seldom on the spot when they are wanted; and besides, Marke, you wouldn't want coppers to keep coming to your premises – it's bad for business. And don't tell me you don't know that!'

As he left I wondered why a man should want to change from a smooth confidence racket which takes brains to operate, into one which is vicious and violent.

Although my flat in Varndell Street was beautifully furnished I didn't always go there to sleep. I had a convertible settee in my office which I would sleep on whenever there had been a long gaming session and I was too tired to go home. I also had a wardrobe with drawers, containing a few suits, shirts and ties, and a dress suit.

Early one afternoon, a few days after I'd shown Gentleman Jim the door, I left the club where I'd slept the night before and went to a restaurant nearby to have something to eat and drink. Dudley, my doorman, who usually slept in the club, had been taken ill and gone to see a doctor. And because some of the members would soon begin to congregate for the afternoon session I left the front door ajar after first locking the door of the office. I had no intention of staying out any longer than forty minutes, and I didn't.

On my return I found the office had been broken into, with splinters lying about on the landing, and every article of clothing gone including a pair of diamond-studded cuff-links, which I usually wore with my dress suit when going to a classy club or theatre. The links were a birthday present from a very good friend of mine, which must have cost her quite a bit. And to crown it all the thief or thieves had the cheek to carry the loot in the two large suitcases which I'd used to carry the goods from my flat.

I reported the matter to the police but though investigations were made, they failed to make an arrest. I didn't connect this with Gentleman Jim at all; in fact he never even entered my mind then.

But suddenly strange things began to happen in the club. Though the club was usually well conducted, since I would not tolerate any bad loser, now every other night there was bound to be someone who would create a lot of noise over nothing; of course he would be slung out and barred altogether from the premises. But the strange thing was all of these troublemakers were white men and none of them were members, and since I couldn't possibly stop a member from bringing in a friend as a guest, this became a problem. Besides, one or two white men would occasionally bluff their way in by telling the doorman that they were with ' Johnny ' who was upstairs playing and they'd just been out a few minutes ago to buy some cigarettes, or some excuse like that. In such circumstances the doorman would usually let them in without bothering to find out if there was a ' Johnny ' in the house.

Fights – which I suspected were phoneys – began to take place between white men. Although they would always finish up by being thrown out this was no good to me. Besides, I began to fear that one of these nights a heavy loser might lose his temper because of the disturbances and start slashing left and right with his razor. This was a hundred per cent possibility because, even though I am not a bad loser and never have been, I knew how I'd feel if people started causing trouble in a game in which I'd lost a good part of my money, driving away the winners who would be only too glad to get out while winning, leaving me with no chance of recovering my losses. And if any serious bloodshed took place I would be finished because the police would close up the place for all time. With this in mind I was thinking of getting all the white men barred except my own personal friends, when a very strange thing happened.

It was a Saturday night and an unusually big dice game was in session in the room on the third floor. I was in the hallway on the ground floor walking towards the billiard room when the front door bell rang. I stopped to see the doorman shuffling towards the door to open it. But before it was half opened about a dozen police officers, including an inspector in uniform, pushed him aside and rushed the premises. Without taking the slightest notice of me they brushed past, running up the stairway two steps at a time.

This was a police raid and they knew exactly where to go. There was nothing strange about a raid. It had happened umpteen times before, and I'd been expecting it because it was due. After all, they had a job to do and the unusual and remarkable protection they had given me was over and I knew it. But I had made up my mind after the last raid that they were never going to catch me red-handed again in a dice game; I had installed a special light in the dice room which, in the event of a raid, would flash whenever the button was pressed. The push-button was placed near to the entrance of the billiard room and was cleverly camouflaged. Operating this was part of the doorman's job, but since I happened to be standing near it I simply placed a hand behind my back and kept pushing the button on and off while the police ran up the stairs.

With a clever smile on my face I watched the back of the last officer disappear up the staircase. I knew that by the time they got to the third floor and burst into the dice room all they would see would be men sitting quietly and innocently reading their magazines and chatting to each other, with the two croupiers playing billiards on the half-sized billiard table which a moment before had been surrounded by dice players. I winked knowingly at the doorman and began to climb up the stairs.

When I entered the dice room I was faced with a sight I could never forget. All the gamblers were standing around the billiard table with an expression of shock printed all over their faces. But none was more shocked than I was. In front of the two croupiers, facing each other on the opposite sides of the long end of the table, were piles of £1 and £5 notes and piles of silver.

Spread eagled on each end of the table, fingers of each hand set wide apart and on top of the two piles of money, were two police officers; the rest of the officers were ordering the men to empty their pockets for further evidence. Never have I seen so much evidence staring me in the face.

Dozens of frantic pairs of eyes stared at me as I entered the room. Another six pairs of eyes glared at me with hate and suspicion as if I had double-crossed them. These six men had all been bound over for twelve months, for the sum of £50. The time had not yet elapsed, which meant that they would have to forfeit that amount, apart from the present trouble they now found themselves in.

But I was in a worse situation than they were. I was the proprietor. The law took a dim view of dice games because they rightly believed it was a hundred per cent game of chance, and though the magistrates might let one off lightly when charged with running a card game, they would take a tough line if the game was dice. I was extremely perplexed. I couldn't understand why they had allowed themselves to be caught red-handed after all the signals I'd given them from the ground floor. This was indeed strange, very strange. And later I was to find out the reason.

The inspector produced his warrant, which I was too confused to ask for. I wouldn't even look at it; what was the difference? Soon we were all shepherded into the waiting police vans and driven to Bow Street police station.

Two hours later I was given bail. Back at the club I examined the warning gadget and discovered that the wire had been neatly severed and pinned down with a piece of dark-coloured paper glued over the area.

Now that I knew it was no accident my mind flashed back

to Gentleman Jim – even though I knew he had never been back on the premises since I showed him the door.

Next morning we appeared before the late Sir Bertram Watson, the chief magistrate at Bow Street police court. I was charged with keeping a common gaming house and the others with being unlawfully found on a gaming premises. Naturally, I pleaded guilty. What with all that evidence I couldn't do otherwise.

I was sentenced to four months' imprisonment; I didn't like this at all. I wouldn't have minded paying the usual big fine, which was the customary procedure if the game played was dice, but a jail sentence – though not unusual – was not to my liking. Gambling or running a gambling game was something I would never accept as a crime. I knew it was against the law, but so what! Everybody gambles now and then, even if only to put a shilling each way on a horse or play the stock market. Life itself is a gamble. No, I didn't like this prison sentence at all! And I mumbled some unprintable words to myself. Sir Bertram must have been a lip reader. He looked hard at me.

As I was being led away Sir Bertram's last comment before the sentence was passed rushed through my mind:

'This is not the first time you have been here for this offence. If I had my way I would deport you back to your own country.' Or words to that effect.

This was something else I didn't like. But I was not in a position to answer back. Yet neither he nor anybody else could stop me thinking.

'My country!' I thought. 'Why, he doesn't know what the hell he is talking about. I am a British subject, and this is my country. I've been here practically all my life.'

When my lawyer came down into the cell to see me, I asked him to apply for an appeal on the ground of sentence, and also apply for bail while he was at it. An hour later I was out and free for the time being. The case went to the London session, but I was only wasting my time and money. Four months it was.

While I was inside I began to think: the club was in Gerrard Street, and Gerrard Street was on the precincts of Bow Street police court. And Sir Bertram Watson would be sitting at Bow Street police court most of the time, if not all of it. In the event of another raid, which was sure to be, what was going to stop Sir Bertram from repeating the sentence? Perhaps even more next time, especially since I had lost my appeal. With this in mind I decided that when I came out I would close up, sell the lease of the premises and look for another place far away from the precincts of Bow Street police court.

Then I thought of his comment about deporting me back to my country if he had his way, and I toyed with the idea of returning to Africa of my own free will. Africa was steaming with the consciousness of nationalism. I would go and help to stoke it up! I had always been politically minded, and this was as good a time as any to go and do something about it.

I felt that I didn't owe Sir Bertram and Britain anything, neither did Africa and her people. I felt I wasn't a criminal, yet I was sent to prison for a common offence which I'd committed in England after the First World War when my colour had prevented me from obtaining work of any kind, even after I'd just served the country. Yes, I would go back. I had never felt so bad, I wanted to revolt against anything and everything.

In prison, however, my passion waned. When I came out I sold the lease of the premises including the furniture, packed up that line of business and went back on the markets and race courses, doing a cabaret occasionally in night clubs. Sometimes I would take a job in the summer as a spieler in a side show as I did in 1951 and 1952 at Bellevue Gardens, Manchester, and also at Dreamland Park, Margate 1956. In the summer of 1953 at the Temple of Mystery, Battersea Park Fun Fair, I doubled up as a magician on the stage and a spieler on the rostrum outside the theatre. It was hard work. But I didn't mind, and I soon realized that I was no longer young or energetic enough to return to Africa in search of Political Justice.

9

I SETTLE DOWN

I had a little windfall in the autumn of 1953 after the fun fair at Battersea Park had closed for the season. Since I had begun to get tired running around in circles I decided to invest the money in a club and stay put. But as the sum wasn't large enough to start one on my own, apart from the fact that vacant premises had become exceedingly hard to obtain, I bought a half share of the Jungle Club, on certain conditions. It was a two-room basement affair with kitchen and wc, situated at the top end of Greek Street near to Soho Square. It was owned by a casual friend Jide Thomas the Nigerian, who now runs the Limbo Club further down the same street, in partnership with another Nigerian, a pleasant and unassuming man called Chuku.

I was able to buy the half share only because the club wasn't doing good at the time. I soon improved the business by giving the place a better look and barring the so-called members who were more of a nuisance than an asset to the club. All kinds of characters, black and white, most of them villains, used to come down there. It was for this reason the original name of the club was soon forgotten and 'Jungle' took its place. Among the regulars were some compulsive gamblers.

One such man was Bernie, a stocky West Indian who worked at a small factory nearby. He was two-deck rummy mad and often popped down from his work to see if there was a game on. At the sight of one his eyes would light up and he'd grab a chair like his whole life depended on it. 'Deal me.' If he won within the next twenty minutes or so he'd rush back to work. If not, then it was the end of the day's work. He popped in at midday one Friday and grabbed a chair. Soon he was stone broke after losing £40. It turned out that half of that money was his week's wages and the other £20 had been given to him by his boss to wager on a horse with the local street bookmaker (there were no betting shops then). And when he discovered the horse had won at 10-1 he threw back his head in anguish and howled like a wounded dog. Soon he was banging his head against the stone wall, moaning, 'What kinda luck is this?' I sometimes wondered what story he told his boss when he went back.

Strange as it may seem there were a number of decent people of both sexes who frequented the Jungle, some of them students, honest business people or professional gamblers who were gentle in every respect. One such person was Mercer, a professional gambler who now runs a gaming club in the same building as the Limbo. He is a Jamaican negro, small in stature, very light skinned, and could pass as a Spaniard or Puerto Rican. He once managed Satan Lefty Flyn, the Jamaican welterweight boxer who twice fought the then British welterweight champion, Ernie Roderick, and beat him once; I was one of the front-row viewers at the Albert Hall the night the Jamaican won this fight. Mercer also once managed Buzz, a brilliant up-and-coming Jamaican middleweight boxer, who joined the RAF just as he was reaching his peak and got killed during a bombing raid over Germany. I had always had a sneaking respect for Mercer, if for no other reason than that he was a clever gambler who could take care of himself in any card game. I often felt this respect was mutual, for we never played hard against each other when we happened to meet at a poker game.

There was Betty, quiet, respectable and middle class. She would come down to the club almost every Saturday night. With cigarette dangling from her lips she would quietly pull a chair and play two-deck rummy till the following Monday. She seldom won. She'd suffer in silence as she lost, lighting one cigarette after the other. I often felt sorry for her. But then no one dragged her there. She just loved the game.

There was Bronnie. She'd be a perfect lady one moment and the next she'd be swearing like a trooper. Yet few women could be more generous. She was always ready to help any friend in need, provided it was a genuine case, for she was nobody's fool. But while Betty was a compulsive gambler, Bronnie could take it or leave it.

I was still co-partner at the Jungle when I first became friendly with Elsie, a young red-haired Yorkshire girl, twenty-six years my junior, living in Manchester and sharing a flat with her younger sister Ada after the loss of their mother in Bradford. I had often come across both girls at the home of a family who were mutual friends. This was during the winter of 1952 when I was the floor manager of the then exclusive Forum Club, situated a couple of hundred yards from Manchester University. But I had never spoken to them, apart from the usual salutation. Nor could I have dreamt then that Elsie would one day become my wife and mother of my five children.

The Jungle had closed for the 1954 Christmas holidays and I had gone to Manchester to spend the few days with this family. Though I had been separated from my wife, Alma, for quite some time and was trying to obtain my divorce this had never prevented me from visiting friends in that city. It happened that Elsie was paying this family a visit on this Christmas evening. We all went to a club and finished up in the house of a mutual friend where we drank and danced the whole night. That's how our friendship began. And when Ada joined the air force and went to Singapore, leaving Elsie by herself, she came to London and we began living together – even before we were married.

By mid 1956, a few months before our son Garry was born, the contract of my partnership at the Jungle had expired and soon my money also began to run out. Fortunately there was a job at Dreamland Park, Margate. But this didn't last long since it was only a summer affair. As I could not afford to be idle, since a child was on its way and that would be another mouth to feed, I had to grab hold of the first job that came along. And so I became a boilerman at the Duke of York's

I SETTLE DOWN

headquarters in King's Road, Chelsea. I kept this job up to my retirement in 1968. Nearly twelve years. The bosses of this concern were super – the best I have ever met, from the brigadier down to Reg Gant, the foreman. Perhaps this was partly why I kept the job so long.

When I had to retire they all tried to talk me out of it. I too was sorry for I had come to like the Duke of York's headquarters and everyone who worked in it. But age was creeping on me and I had begun to have attacks of rheumatism. After all, stoking boilers and trimming coke is not exactly a cushy job. I was given a farewell party at the London Irish club in the main building, which was then managed by Andy Riddler and his wife and after the party, which lasted till about 4 am, Andy personally drove me home. Since then not a year has passed without my receiving a Christmas card from Reg Gant and his family, who still live at the Duke of York's. This I greatly appreciate. I am a lucky man.

And when I saw the beautiful bunch of flowers which was delivered to Elsie on the morning of Mother's Day 1974 and realized it was sent all the way from the United States, through Interflora, by our eldest son Garry, now seventeen and serving in the Royal Navy, I felt very proud. I am indeed a lucky man. There have been many ups and downs in my life but I have learnt to take the rough with the smooth and I shall die a happy man.

Since I first came to Great Britain, as a stowaway, all those years ago, I have witnessed a vast number of changes, both in the numbers of coloured people over here, and in people's attitudes. The days when a Liverpool woman could think that a black boy serving at the altar during Mass was a devil are passed, and for the better. True, it has not been easy for the British people to accept large numbers of immigrants, and there are still people who try to whip up unpleasant campaigns to send them home, but in general, people are far more tolerant now than they used to be. It is a change for the better, and I am proud to have spent so much of my life in such a pleasant country.